D1447443

States' Rights

Other Books in the Bill of Rights series:

States' Rights

Jodie Lynn Boduch, Book Editor

GREENHAVEN PRESS
An imprint of Thomson Gale, a part of The Thomson Corporation

Detroit • New York • San Francisco • San Diego • New Haven, Conn.
Waterville, Maine • London • Munich

Bonnie Szumski, *Publisher*
Helen Cothran, *Managing Editor*
Scott Barbour, *Series Editor*

© 2006 Thomson Gale, a part of The Thomson Corporation.

For more information, contact: Greenhaven Press
27500 Drake Rd.
Farmington Hills, MI 48331-3535
Or you can visit our Internet site at http://www.gale.com

LIBRARY OF CONGRESS CATALOGING-IN-PUBLICATION DATA

States' Rights / Jodie Lynn Boduch, book editor
    p. cm. -- (The Bill of rights)
    Includes bibliographical references and index. 0-7377-1935-4 (lib. bdg. : alk. paper)
    1. State Rights--History. 2. Federal government--United States--History.
3. United States. Constitution. 10th Amendment--History. I. Boduch, Jodie Lynn. II. Bill of Rights (San Diego, Calif.)
    JK311.S725 2006
    342.73'042--dc22

                                                          2005054543

Printed in the United States of America
10 9 8 7 6 5 4 3 2 1

Contents

Harlan Fiske Stone

In *United States v. Darby* (1941), the Court overturned *Hammer v. Dagenhart* and ruled that the federal government is authorized to regulate state labor laws.

Chapter 3: Major Conflicts Over States' Rights

In the early 1830s, southern leader John C. Calhoun led a movement championing the right of states to nullify federal laws that the states' citizens deemed unconstitutional.

The secession of the Southern states not only started the Civil War, but it also launched debates about the Constitution, the Union, and state sovereignty.

The civil rights movement gained the support of the federal government, but some states, such as Mississippi, responded by invoking state sovereignty.

Chapter 4: Modern Perspectives on the State-Federal Relationship

The Supreme Court has not interfered in the Massachusetts ruling on same-sex marriage because the federal system respects each state's culture.

In *Raich v. Ashcroft* (2005), the Supreme Court maintained that federal antidrug laws supersede state regulations concerning medical marijuana use.

Foreword

> "I cannot agree with those who think of the Bill of Rights as an 18th century straightjacket, unsuited for this age. . . . The evils it guards against are not only old, they are with us now, they exist today."
>
> Hugo Black, associate justice of the U.S. Supreme Court, 1937–1971

The Bill of Rights codifies the freedoms most essential to American democracy. Freedom of speech, freedom of religion, the right to bear arms, the right to a trial by a jury of one's peers, the right to be free from cruel and unusual punishment—these are just a few of the liberties that the Founding Fathers thought it necessary to spell out in the first ten amendments to the U.S. Constitution.

While the document itself is quite short (consisting of fewer than five hundred words), and while the liberties it protects often seem straightforward, the Bill of Rights has been a source of debate ever since its creation. Throughout American history, the rights the document protects have been tested and reinterpreted. Again and again, individuals perceiving violations of their rights have sought redress in the courts. The courts in turn have struggled to decipher the original intent of the founders as well as the need to accommodate changing societal norms and values.

The ultimate responsibility for addressing these claims has fallen to the U.S. Supreme Court. As the highest court in the nation, it is the Supreme Court's role to interpret the Constitution. The Court has considered numerous cases in which people have accused government of impinging on their rights.

In the process, the Court has established a body of case law and precedents that have, in a sense, defined the Bill of Rights. In doing so, the Court has often reversed itself and introduced new ideas and approaches that have altered the legal meaning of the rights contained in the Bill of Rights. As a general rule, the Court has erred on the side of caution, upholding and expanding the rights of individuals rather than restricting them.

An example of this trend is the definition of cruel and unusual punishment. The Eighth Amendment specifically states, "Excessive bail shall not be required, nor excessive fines imposed, nor cruel and unusual punishments inflicted." However, over the years the Court has had to grapple with defining what constitutes "cruel and unusual punishments." In colonial America, punishments for crimes included branding, the lopping off of ears, and whipping. Indeed, these punishments were considered lawful at the time the Bill of Rights was written. Obviously, none of these punishments are legal today. In order to justify outlawing certain types of punishment that are deemed repugnant by the majority of citizens, the Court has ruled that it must consider the prevailing opinion of the masses when making such decisions. In overturning the punishment of a man stripped of his citizenship, the Court stated in 1958 that it must rely on society's "evolving standards of decency" when determining what constitutes cruel and unusual punishment. Thus the definition of cruel and unusual is not frozen to include only the types of punishment that were illegal at the time of the framing of the Bill of Rights; specific modes of punishment can be rejected as society deems them unjust.

Another way that the Courts have interpreted the Bill of Rights to expand individual liberties is through the process of "incorporation." Prior to the passage of the Fourteenth Amendment, the Bill of Rights was thought to prevent only the federal government from infringing on the rights listed in the document. However, the Fourteenth Amendment, which was passed in the wake of the Civil War, includes the words, " . . . nor shall any state deprive any person of life, liberty, or property, without due process of law; nor deny to any person within its jurisdiction the equal protection of the laws." Citing this passage, the Court has ruled that many of the liberties contained in the Bill of Rights apply to state and local governments as well as the federal government. This process of incorporation laid the legal foundation for the civil rights movement—most specifically the 1954 *Brown v. Board of Education* ruling that put an end to legalized segregation.

As these examples reveal, the Bill of Rights is not static. It truly is a living document that is constantly being reinterpreted and redefined. The Bill of Rights series captures this vital aspect of one of America's most cherished founding texts. Each volume in the series focuses on one particular right protected in the Bill of Rights. Through the use of primary and secondary sources, the right's evolution is traced from colonial times to the present. Primary sources include landmark Supreme Court rulings, speeches by prominent experts, and editorials. Secondary sources include historical analyses, law journal articles, book excerpts, and magazine articles. Each book also includes several features to facilitate research, including a bibliography, an annotated table of contents, an annotated list of relevant Supreme Court cases, an introduction, and an index. These elements help to make the Bill of Rights series a fascinating and useful tool for examining the fundamental liberties of American democracy.

Introduction

Many of the Founding Fathers viewed the Tenth Amendment, the last amendment in the Bill of Rights, as the keystone in the whole structure. Its importance is made clear by the fact that it was the only section of the Bill of Rights that was proposed by all of the state conventions that recommended amendments to the original Constitution. As the Constitution had been written and ratified, the debate over the relative powers of the state and federal governments had been intense. In the end the Federalists, who had advocated a strong federal government, had emerged victorious. The Anti-Federalists feared that the strong federal government created by the Constitution could trample on the right of the states to govern themselves as they chose. By declaring that the "powers not delegated to the United States by the Constitution, nor prohibited by it to the States, are reserved to the States respectively, or to the people," the Tenth Amendment was meant to reassure Anti-Federalists that the states retained many of the powers that they had previously enjoyed under the Articles of Confederation.

In addition to formally acknowledging the states' power to govern, the Tenth Amendment also was seen as an additional protector of individual rights. The states, having been allowed to retain their independence, could be the guardians of their own citizens' rights, even against a powerful federal government trying to usurp them. The Tenth Amendment could be the real bulwark for the other nine amendments, providing added weight to all their grand pronouncements of individual rights.

A Quiet Amendment

Despite its seeming importance, however, the Tenth Amendment has not featured prominently in Supreme Court decisions. The Court has wrestled again and again with the meaning of the First Amendment's guarantee of free speech, the Fourth Amendment's protection from unfair searches and seizures, and the Eighth Amendment's prohibition of cruel and unusual punishments, to name just a few examples. In contrast, the Court has been relatively silent, sometimes even contemptuous and dismissive, when it comes to the meaning of the Tenth Amendment. In the landmark 1819 case of *McCullough v. Maryland*, for example, Chief Justice John Marshall declared that the Tenth Amendment was framed merely "for the purpose of quieting the excessive jealousies which had been excited" during the debate between the Federalists and Anti-Federalists.

The Court has not always embraced this view, but in many cases involving states' rights, the Tenth Amendment has played a surprisingly minor role. The cases defining the powers and privileges of the states rest instead on the Fourteenth Amendment and the "commerce clause" of the original Constitution. Passed in the wake of the Civil War, the Fourteenth Amendment forbade state governments from passing laws that violated "the privileges or immunities of citizens" or that deprived persons of "due process of law." After lying virtually dormant for decades, the Fourteenth Amendment eventually provided the basis for a significant increase in the power of the federal government in relation to the states.

In 1873, within five years of its passage, the Supreme Court ruled against an expansive interpretation of the Fourteenth Amendment in the very influential Slaughterhouse Cases. In rejecting a federal lawsuit against a monopoly set up by the state of Louisiana, the Court found that the Fourteenth Amendment could not be used to expand federal power in the area of commerce. In his majority opinion, Justice Samuel F. Miller wrote that any alternative interpretation "radically changes the whole theory of the relations of the State and

Federal governments to each other and of both these governments to the people."

Expanding Federal Power

In the wake of the upheavals brought on by the Great Depression of the 1930s and President Franklin D. Roosevelt's attempts to restore America's economy, the Supreme Court began to reexamine earlier assumptions regarding state-federal relations. Ultimately the Court ruled that Congress's power to regulate interstate commerce gave it broad authority over numerous issues that could theoretically have an impact on commerce between states, such as minimum wages, maximum hours, and other labor laws. Since then, the commerce clause has been used to justify numerous labor, environmental, and other regulations that impact the states, although the Court has on occasion struck down federal legislation that seemed to overstretch the definition of interstate commerce.

Along with broadening its application of the commerce clause, the Court also began to reexamine the Fourteenth Amendment's guarantees of rights and privileges. In a series of rulings beginning in the 1930s, the Court incorporated many of the provisions of the Bill of Rights into the Fourteenth Amendment; that is, it declared that most, although not all, of the rights protected in the Bill of Rights applied to state governments as well as the federal government. Whereas the Court had previously limited itself to monitoring only the actions of the federal government, it now began to examine the constitutionality of state laws, greatly increasing the federal government's power over state governments.

Perhaps the most dramatic outcome of this new interpretation of the Fourteenth Amendment was the success of the civil rights movement. Developments such as the 1954 *Brown v. Board of Education* decision, which outlawed school segregation; the Civil Rights Act of 1964, which outlawed discrimination in housing and employment; and the Voting Rights Act of 1965, which helped to secure minorities' access to the polls, all depended on this new view of the Fourteenth Amendment. Along with the judicial branch, the legislative and executive branches of the federal government embraced a view of civil rights that transcended the traditional view of states' rights and dismantled the entire system of segregation that had grown up over nearly a century. A particular view of federalism was decisively overturned, and because southern leaders used the rallying cry of "states' rights" to resist integration, the phrase acquired racist undertones that continue to trouble its supporters today.

An Orphan Amendment

Together, the new interpretations of the commerce clause and the Fourteenth Amendment have created the modern view that gives the federal government far more latitude in defending the rights of citizens against their own state legislatures. In the process, the Tenth Amendment has been largely overlooked. While most of the other amendments have generated intense debate both inside and outside the Supreme Court, discussion of the Tenth Amendment is relatively rare. The amendment that was to guarantee the rights of states and, in doing so, the rights of all their citizens, instead remains something of an orphan, holding out a principle that many embrace in the abstract without really controlling the decisions of the Supreme Court or animating the emotions of the American people.

The Bill of Rights

CHAPTER 1

Early Debates Regarding State and Federal Powers

The Creation of the Tenth Amendment

Charles F. Hobson

The framers of the Constitution first met in 1787; in 1789 the federal republic of the United States of America came into existence. The two years in between were marked by elaborate discussions at each of the state conventions concerning various points of the proposed constitution. One issue that came up repeatedly was states' rights. This controversial question led to a number of debates and resulted in the Tenth Amendment of the Bill of Rights.

In the following excerpt historian Charles Hobson traces the debates over the balance of power between the federal government and the states. He also describes the respective positions of the two main camps of opposing thought: the Federalists and the Anti-Federalists. Whereas Federalists maintained that a national union would solidify the independence of the states, Anti-Federalists expressed fears that a federal government would trample on the liberty of the states and the people. Ultimately, the Tenth Amendment addresses the relationship between the states and the federal government in a manner that leaves room for interpretation. Hobson concludes that the federal republic created by the Constitution represented a true middle ground between the Federalist and Anti-Federalist points of view.

Charles F. Hobson is a PhD with a specialization in American legal and constitutional history. The author of a book on nineteenth-century chief justice John Marshall, Hobson is also an editor and history lecturer at the College of William and Mary in Williamsburg, Virginia.

Charles F. Hobson, *The Bill of Rights: A Lively Heritage*, edited by Jon Kukla. Richmond: Virginia State Library and Archives, 1987. Copyright © 1987 by The Library of Virginia. All Rights Reserved. Reproduced by permission.

T he Tenth Amendment seems different from the other nine. It speaks not of safeguards for the *rights* of individual citizens but of the distribution of *powers* between the United States and the states or people. In the twentieth century, when judicial enforcement of the Bill of Rights often voids state laws or state court decisions that violate individual rights, this reserved powers amendment has served as a text for the assertion of state rights against the spirit of the Bill of Rights. In 1789, however, the reserved powers amendment was recognized as an essential part of the Bill of Rights. Of all the amendments proposed for the Constitution, none was more frequently recommended: seven state ratifying conventions, along with the minority of the Pennsylvania convention, called for an explicit declaration reserving to the states the powers not delegated to the general government. Setting limits on the exercise of power by the federal government was to Samuel Adams "a summary of a bill of rights."

A Defeat for the Antifederalists

In 1789, few Americans expected any danger that the states would violate fundamental liberties. Amendments protecting individual rights were intended to restrict only the federal government; an amendment reserving undelegated powers to the states simply reinforced the guarantees of personal liberty found in the state declarations of rights. The omission of a bill of rights was not the only reason Antifederalists opposed the Constitution in 1788 and 1789. Their demand for a bill of rights was but one part—and by no means the most important part—of their campaign to alter the Constitution in the direction of the discarded Articles of Confederation. They wished to restore the sovereignty of the states, the foundation of the old system, by limiting the central government's substantive powers over taxation, commerce, and treaty making.

The Antifederalists won protections for individual rights, but they failed in their larger aim. The enactment of the Bill of Rights was, in truth, a bitter disappointment, a second and decisive defeat for the unreconciled opponents of the Constitution. Friends of the Constitution, at first hostile to a bill of rights, preempted the campaign for amendments and turned it to their own purposes. Credit for this brilliant political statesmanship belongs to James Madison, who drafted the amendments and then shepherded them through Congress. Madison saw an opportunity to appease the large group of Americans who except for its omission of a bill of rights favored the Constitution. The addition of a bill of rights, he shrewdly calculated, would separate the well-meaning from the hostile critics and broaden popular support of the Constitution without sacrificing anything essential to the power and energy of the new government.

Creating a New Federalism

Like the first nine amendments, the Tenth Amendment directly answered fears that the proposed national government would destroy the state governments. The Antifederalists saw no other way to unite the states than in a league of free and equal states, each retaining full sovereignty, like the Articles of Confederation. Strictly speaking, the Confederation Congress was not a government but an instrument subordinate to the states for specific military and diplomatic objectives. It acted through the states, not directly upon individual citizens, and passed resolutions and ordinances but not laws. Law-making authority—sovereignty—remained with the states. There was no national executive or judiciary.

In practice the states under the Confederation were not completely sovereign, and Congress did act like a real government in war and diplomacy. Yet the experience of the American Revolution did not alter the essential structure of the Confederation as a league of independent states (the commonly accepted definition of a "federal" policy). The second article of the Confederation declared that "each state retains its sovereignty, freedom and independence, and every Power, Jurisdiction and right, which is not by this confederation expressly delegated to the United States, in Congress assembled." This article, a perfect summary of the federal system of the Confederation, was the parent of the Tenth Amendment. The offspring, however, has no mention of the "sovereignty, freedom and independence" of the states. Significantly missing, too, is the word "expressly" before "delegated." The Tenth Amendment, so it seemed, was a husk without a kernel. Its framers, to be sure, had consciously conformed the second article to the spirit of the new Constitution. As the second article expressed the "old" federalism of the Confederation, so the Tenth Amendment expressed the "new" federalism of the Constitution.

The most striking change proposed by the Constitution was the creation of a real central government with legislative, executive, and judicial departments. A republican government like those of the states, it would embrace the whole United States, deriving its powers from the people and acting directly upon them. The American people henceforth would be citizens of two governments, each with its proper sphere. Sovereignty was divided between a central government with jurisdiction over the entire nation and state governments with local jurisdiction. The Constitution embodied a new definition of *federalism*, the one we are familiar with today in our civics textbooks.

Antifederalist Concerns

Antifederalists who indicted the Constitution for its vague, equivocal expressions applied the same charge to the final text of the Tenth Amendment, which did nothing to clarify the meaning of the Constitution. The difference between the second article of the Confederation and the Tenth Amendment to the Constitution was the difference between the old federalism and the new. It was a measure of the political distance

Americans had traveled since 1776, of how they had transformed their ways of thinking about "federalism," "sovereignty," and "republican" government. The heart of the Antifederalists' critique of the Constitution was their adamant refusal to surrender the old federalism of the Articles of Confederation. They claimed to be the true spokesmen for federalism; they denied that the Constitution was *federal* in the accepted meaning of the word; and they denounced the friends of the plan for appropriating the *Federalist* label. This confusion of political terminology, Antifederalists said, masked a conspiracy to replace the state governments with a consolidated national government and suppress the rights and liberties of the people.

For all their exaggerated rhetoric, the Antifederalists correctly perceived that the Constitution was a radical departure from their existing government. The framers offered a government that defied precise description: a strange, unwieldy hybrid of a unitary government and a confederacy of state governments without precedent in history or in the writings of the ablest philosophers. Luther Martin, of Maryland, expressed the bewilderment of the Antifederalists when he protested that he was unable to discover

> anything in the history of mankind or in the sentiments of those who have favoured the world with their ideas on government, to warrant or countenance the motley mixture of a system proposed: a system which is an innovation in government of the most extraordinary kind; a system neither wholly federal, nor wholly national—but a strange hotchpotch of both.

Federalists, too, described the plan as "partly federal, and partly national" to reassure the people that the states would continue to be essential parts of the system and that the federal features would predominate. These assurances fell upon deaf ears among Antifederalists who insisted that a government could either be federal or consolidated but not both.

The Constitution, they said, unmistakably "squinted" in the latter direction.

Consolidation and Tyranny

Consolidation was a word Antifederalists repeatedly used against the Constitution. What did they mean? And why did they regard it as dangerous? Consolidated governments held supreme political and legal authority within their jurisdictions. In this sense state governments with no federal relationships to their counties, townships, or cities were consolidated governments. The alarming implication of the Constitution was that the states would be reduced to the petty status of counties and corporations. Antifederalists took no comfort in knowing that the proposed new government was republican in form, for they contended that any government with such an extensive territory as the United States would necessarily degenerate into monarchy or despotism. While the friends of the Constitution repeatedly argued that it was both federal and republican, Antifederalists saw only consolidation and eventual tyranny.

Consolidation pervaded the whole system, beginning with the opening words of the preamble: "The question turns, sir, on that poor little thing—the expression, We, the *people*, instead of the *states*, of America," said Patrick Henry at the Virginia Convention of 1788. This preamble betrayed an intention to make "this alarming transition, from a confederacy to a consolidated government." To Pennsylvania Antifederalist Robert Whitehill these words showed that "the old foundation of the union is destroyed, the principle of confederation excluded, and a new and unwieldy system of consolidated empire is set up, upon the ruins of the present compact between the states."

Then, if further proof were needed that the framers intended [in the words of John Smilie] "to absorb and abolish the efficient sovereignty and independent powers of the several States, in order to invigorate and aggrandize the general government," one only had to turn to the body of the Constitution. Powers of the central government were stated in general terms that left opportunity for expansion by interpretation or implication. The power to levy taxes and raise armies— the purse and sword—were themselves sufficient to destroy the states, and the clause giving Congress power to pass all laws "necessary and proper" seemed to give the legislature authority to do whatever it wished. Under close scrutiny by the Antifederalists, every clause of the Constitution seemed calculated toward a consolidated government that would leave the states as subordinate administrative units only. Who could misunderstand a statement that the Constitution and the laws and treaties made under it would be the [according to Smilie] "supreme law," state constitutions and laws "to the contrary notwithstanding" ?

The Place of Sovereignty

All these objections to the Constitution rested on the Antifederalists' belief that, sovereignty being indivisible, the Federalists' claim that the Constitution distributed portions of sovereign power between the general and state governments was absurd. Did not all the respected political thinkers agree that there could be only one supreme law-making authority in a state? It was inconceivable that one government could exist within another ("*imperium in imperio*" [an empire within an empire]), said William Grayson, of Virginia; the absurdity surpassed "everything that I have read of concerning other governments." "The idea of two distinct sovereigns in the same country, separately *possessed* of sovereign and supreme power, in the same matters at the same time," a New York Antifederalist sneered, "is as supreme an absurdity, as that two distinct separate circles can be bounded exactly by the same circumference."

Such logic left no middle ground. Either the general government or the states would predominate, and the tendency of the Constitution left no doubt where supremacy would eventually reside. The minority of the Pennsylvania convention believed

> that two co-ordinate sovereignties would be a solecism in politics; that . . . it would be contrary to the nature of things that both should exist together—one or the other would necessarily triumph in the fulness of dominion. However, the contest could not be of long continuance, as the State governments are divested of every means of defence, and will be obliged by "the supreme law of the land" *to yield at discretion.*

The doctrine of sovereignty proved that the Constitution "was calculated to abolish entirely the state governments, and to melt down the states into one entire government" [according to Robert Yates].

Redefining Sovereignty

[French Englightenment thinker Charles de Secondat, Baron de] Montesquieu's idea that republican government was suitable only for small territories with homogeneous populations gave Antifederalists additional reasons to worry about consolidated government. "Is it to be supposed," asked George Mason, author of the Virginia Declaration of Rights,

> that one national government will suit so extensive a territory, embracing so many climates, and containing inhabitants, so very different in manners, habits, and customs? It is ascertained by history, that there never was a government, over a very extensive country, without destroying the liberties of the people.

The minority in the Pennsylvania convention dissented from the Constitution because it was "the opinion of the most celebrated writers on government, and confirmed by uniform ex-

The signing of the U.S. Constitution in 1787. © Bettmann/CORBIS

perience, that a very extensive territory cannot be governed on the principles of freedom, otherwise than by a confederation of republics." How could such a government simultaneously represent the interests of New England farmers, New York merchants, Pennsylvania artisans, and South Carolina planters? First the national government would degenerate into a type appropriate for an extensive territory—either monarchy or despotism. Then, unity would require military coercion and the dreaded scourge of free governments—a standing army—would be needed to enforce obedience to the general government. In short, the reasoning went, the proposed national government could not possibly remain republican. To the Antifederalists, the Constitution could have but one result: the annihilation of the states and the accompanying destruction of the rights and liberties of the people.

To explain the new system's "strange hotch-potch" of federal and national features, the Federalists modified the idea that sovereignty was indivisible. Unlike the Antifederalists, who equated sovereignty with government, the Federalists asserted that ultimate power resided not with the general or state governments but with the people themselves. The people could allocate portions of their undivided supreme authority to be exercised by different governments. This redefinition of sovereignty, which had emerged during the period of constitution making and political experimentation between 1776 and 1787, made possible the new federalism of the Constitution.

The Practicality of Republican Government

Popular sovereignty had been largely an abstraction in 1776. In practice, in the act of forming their governments the people had always surrendered power to them. During the American Revolution, however, the novel concept of the people actively exercising power "out of doors" developed. The most important tangible form of this idea was the convention of the people. By writing a constitution in a general convention and by ratifying it in special conventions, the people truly acted as the "constituent power" and wrote their own fundamental laws. According to this new way of thinking, the people did not surrender ultimate power when forming governments. The Constitution became the concrete expression of their permanent claim of supreme authority. The people, said James Wilson, of Pennsylvania, "can distribute one portion of power to the more contracted circle called State governments; they can also furnish another proportion to the government of the United States." The powers of each were only "so many emanations of power from the people." Federalists argued that this relocation, or restoration, of sovereignty in the people answered the charge of consolidation, for both the general and state governments were held in check by the will of the people embodied in the Constitution.

The Antifederalist objection that republican government was practicable only in small territories had, in truth, been undermined by the factious politics of the state governments since 1776. Republican government as exercised in the states had come to mean government by majority factions whose laws reflected narrow self-interests rather than the public good. James Madison observed in *The Federalist*, No. 10, that the very smallness of the state jurisdictions had made it relatively easy for factions to gain control. His solution to the problem of faction was not to abandon principle but to enlarge the jurisdiction: "Extend the sphere, and you take in a greater variety of parties and interests; you make it less probable that a majority of the whole will have a common motive to invade the rights of other citizens." Madison's great insight was to realize that enlarging the republic could promote moderation and justice. By distributing powers and functions between the general and state governments, the new federalism made it feasible to enlarge the jurisdiction of a republic. "And happily for the *republican cause*," he wrote, "the practicable sphere [of republican government] may be carried to very great extent, by a judicious modification and mixture of the *federal principle*." The new federalism of the Constitution provided "a Republican remedy for the diseases most incident to Republican Government." Just as the notion of divided sovereignty gave new meaning to federalism, so the redefinition of federalism made possible the reformation of republican government.

The Foundation of a Bill of Rights

These fundamentally different assumptions held by the Federalists and Antifederalists shaped their quarrel over the necessity of a bill of rights. Seizing upon the new conception of sovereignty, Federalists such as James Wilson contended that the government under the Constitution was only a partial delegation of the people's original supreme power and, therefore, adding a bill of rights would be "superfluous and absurd." Retaining everything not delegated, said Alexander Hamilton, "the people surrender nothing; and as they retain every thing, they have no need of particular reservations." Adhering to the traditional notion of sovereignty, Antifederalists found this stock reply unacceptable. They warned that the people delegated all "rights not expressly reserved" (a principle that had made state declarations of rights necessary) and that the proposed federal government was in this respect no different from the states. Antifederalists thought that an explicit reservation of powers to the states was the most effective guarantee for individual liberty. If the Constitution had included an express reservation in terms similar to the second article of the Confederation, North Carolinian Samuel Spencer concluded, "it would have superseded the necessity of a bill of rights."

Thus, the reserved powers amendment was the very foundation of a bill of rights. By agreeing to amend the Constitution to safeguard individual rights, the Federalists wisely sacrificed their theory to keep the Constitution's original delegation of powers intact. The legislative history of the Tenth Amendment illustrates this fact. James Madison presented a declaration of reserved powers to the House of Representatives in June 1789 that read: "The powers not delegated by this Constitution, nor prohibited by it to the states, are reserved to the States respectively." In his accompanying speech the Virginia representative noted that several state ratifying conventions were

> particularly anxious that it should be declared in the constitution, that the powers not therein delegated, should be reserved to the several states. Perhaps words which may define this more precisely, than the whole of the instrument now does, may be considered as superfluous. I admit they may be deemed unnecessary; but there can be no harm in making such a declaration, if gentlemen will allow that the fact is as stated. I am sure I understand it so, and do therefore propose it.

Madison cleverly implied that his draft reflected the wording recommended by the state conventions. In fact, most of those conventions copied the second article of the Confederation by reserving all powers not "expressly delegated." Madison deliberately omitted "expressly," for he intended the amendment only as an explicit statement of a principle that he regarded as implied in the original Constitution.

The Importance of "Expressly"

The significance Madison attached to "expressly" was revealed in a brief debate in the committee of the whole on 18 August when Thomas Tudor Tucker, of South Carolina, moved to add the word. Madison immediately objected that "it was impossible to confine a government to the exercise of express powers. There must necessarily be admitted powers by implication, unless the constitution descended to recount every minutiæ." The doctrine of implied powers, which Madison fully accepted, would have been foreclosed from the beginning. Years later Chief Justice John Marshall confirmed Madison's understanding of the omission of "expressly." The Constitution, said Marshall, contained no phrase

> which, like the articles of confederation, excludes incidental or implied powers; and which requires that every thing granted shall be expressly and minutely described. Even the 10th amendment, which was framed for the purpose of quieting the excessive jealousies which had been excited, omits the word "expressly." . . . The men who drew and adopted this amendment had experienced the embarrassments resulting from the insertion of this word in the articles of confederation, and probably omitted it to avoid those embarrassments.

On 21 August, Elbridge Gerry, of Massachusetts, again moved for "expressly." The motion lost on a roll-call vote, thirty-two to seventeen. Three days later the House adopted the reserved powers amendment as written by Madison. When the amendments were taken up by the Senate, that body on 7 September defeated a third and final attempt to insert "expressly." Two days later the reserved powers amendment passed the Senate in the form that Congress formally approved on 25 September 1789 and sent to the states for ratification: "The powers not delegated to the United States by the Constitution, nor prohibited by it to the States, are reserved to the States respectively, or to the people." The Senate had added two phrases to the amendment: "to the United States" and "or to the people." The reasons for these additions were not recorded (for the Senate then met behind closed doors), but a few conjectures may be offered to suggest why they were made. The additional words gave balance and symmetry not only to the amendment itself but also to its relationship with the Constitution as a whole. The final wording explicitly recognized the three constituent elements of the new American federalism— the United States, the states, and the people—and the inclusion of "or to the people" reaffirmed the distinction that was central to this new definition of popular sovereignty. Fittingly, too, this change meant that a document that opened with "We the people" now concluded with "the people."

The Tenth Amendment's Purpose

The Tenth Amendment offered cold comfort to the Antifederalists for it did little to remove the specter of consolidation. Yet these "men of little faith" [in the words of twentieth-century political scientist Cecelia Kenyon] were more successful than they realized. In the debate over the Constitution, they had compelled the Federalists to deny consolidation and to explain a new federalism in which both the national and state governments were subordinate to the supreme authority of the people. This process of explaining the Constitution to make it acceptable to the American people and consistent with their historical experience effectively foreclosed the possibility of a unitary national government for the United States. As a declaration of the "federal" construction of the Constitution, the Tenth Amendment *was* in one sense superfluous, as

Madison had said, but only because its purpose had been accomplished in the clarification of terms by which the Constitution was presented and justified to the people before its enactment.

Contrary to the worst fears of the Antifederalists, the federal republic that came into being in 1789 represented a true middle ground between consolidation and a confederacy of sovereign states. The nature of the relationship between the federal and state governments was not clear in 1789 and would never be fully clarified. The Tenth Amendment, as Marshall observed, left "the question, whether the particular power which may become the subject of contest has been delegated to the one government, or prohibited to the other, to depend on a fair construction of the whole instrument."

The Constitution, as subsequent events have shown, is ambiguous enough to support almost diametrically opposing constructions. Over the course of two centuries it has been invoked both to enlarge and to restrict the scope of national powers. Interestingly, when the Tenth Amendment has been cited to narrow the scope of federal power, judges have frequently altered its text by interpolating "expressly." While the net result since 1789, and especially since 1865, has been a vast increase in the powers and jurisdiction of the national government, the system is still recognizably federal. The Tenth Amendment stands as a constant reminder, if one is needed, that political authority in the United States is not concentrated in one central government but divided and dispersed among many jurisdictions.

The States' Rights Debate from Colonial Times to the Early Nineteenth Century

Richard E. Ellis

In the following excerpt historian Richard E. Ellis traces the origins of states' rights arguments and examines the way these arguments evolved in subsequent decades. His analysis concludes at the start of Andrew Jackson's two-term presidency in 1828. In the colonial era, Ellis writes, decentralized government was preferred due to the diversity of the colonies and their distrust of the British monarchy. Although the colonists banded together to defeat the British, opposition to a strong central government remained strong after the Revolution. During the subsequent decades, Ellis writes, the debate over the relative power of the federal and state governments represented a division in the nation between elites and agrarians. Elites favored a strong central government, whereas agrarians preferred more local control.

Richard E. Ellis, professor of history at State University of New York at Buffalo, is the author of two books as well as a number of book chapters and journal articles. His research interests include American constitutional history and the early republic.

For nearly a half-century following independence in 1776 the central constitutional issue in America was the problem of the distribution of power between the states and the national government. In one form or another the issue of states' rights permeated almost all ideological and political discussions of the antebellum era. Scholars have long recognized this, and there has been considerable work done on the

Richard E. Ellis, *The Union at Risk: Jacksonian Democracy, States' Rights, and the Nullification Crisis*. New York: Oxford University Press, 1987. Copyright © 1987 by Richard Ellis. Reproduced by permission of Oxford University Press, Inc.

specific events in which the concept of states' rights has manifested itself: the writing of the Articles of Confederation, the debate over the creation and adoption of the United States Constitution, the Kentucky and Virginia Resolutions, Federalist opposition during the administrations of Thomas Jefferson and James Madison, the various criticisms of the Supreme Court's nationalist decisions during the 1820s, Andrew Jackson's numerous vetoes, South Carolina's nullification of the tariffs of 1828 and 1832, the problem of slavery, and the secession crisis culminating in the Civil War and the Reconstruction of the Union. Yet surprisingly little has been done to look at the states' rights argument itself very closely, to try to explain its origins and its evolution in early American history, or the different ways in which the argument has been used at different points in time.

The Colonial Cultural Heritage

The sources of the states' rights argument that emerged in the years immediately after 1776 were complex and many. In part it can be traced back to the colonists' cultural heritage, since throughout the sixteenth, seventeenth, and even eighteenth centuries, opposition to the centralizing tendency of the monarchy was a way of life for many people. Also of great significance were the separate and independent ways in which the individual colonies were settled and developed and the various commercial rivalries, political jealousies, and other petty hostilities that undermined almost all attempts to get them to cooperate with each other before the Revolutionary crisis began. Looking back at the successful rebellion against British authority that began in 1776, John Adams viewed it as something of a miracle, since before that—

> The colonies had grown up under constitutions of government so different, there was so great a variety of religions, they were composed of so many different nations, their customs, manners, and habits had so little resemblance, and

their intercourse had been so rare, and their knowledge of each other so imperfect, that to unite them in the same principles in theory and the same system of action, was certainly a very difficult enterprise. The complete accomplishment of it, in so short a time and by such simple means, was perhaps a singular example in the history of Mankind. Thirteen clocks were made to strike together. A perfection of mechanism, which no artist had ever before effected.

The Revolution both undermined and reinforced the centrifugal heritage of the colonial period. It undermined it by forcing Americans to band together successfully to fight a common foe, and, of course, in the process many people from different parts of the country came to realize that they had a great deal in common. Unquestionably, a spirit of nationalism and with it a desire to see the creation of a strong and active central government were real and dynamic results of the Revolution and suffused the feelings and thoughts of such important figures as George Washington, Alexander Hamilton, John Marshall, Robert Morris, John Adams, Thomas Jefferson, and James Madison. But just as strong were those dimensions of the Revolution that did not lend support to any program that would weaken local authority, particularly by the creation of a strong central government. The debate between Americans and Englishmen in the years immediately before 1776 focused on the rights of the colonies as opposed to those of the imperial government. The Revolution, after all, was fought to deny the authority of the only central government that the colonists had ever known: Great Britain. For most Americans, therefore, in the years immediately following independence, it was natural to associate the idea of a central government with England's arbitrary actions during the 1760s and 1770s.

Conditions for Localism

Buttressing and giving direction to this experience was the ideology of the Revolution, which stressed the tension and essential incompatibility between liberty and power. The weak central government created by the Articles of Confederation, despite the objections of some spokesman from the Middle Atlantic states, seemed to flow almost naturally from the heritage of the colonial period and the intellectual thrust of the Revolution.

After 1776 a related but nonetheless distinct source of support for the decentralization of authority came from those who wished to see the democratic potential of the Revolution fulfilled. Viewing government as at best a necessary evil, determined to protect the rights of the governed from subversion by their rulers and suspicious of any kind of institutional arrangement that placed excessive power in the hands of the few, many people believed government should be made as weak, as simple, and as immediately and directly responsible to the will of the majority as possible. For these reasons eighteenth-century democrats favored such devices as broad suffrage, annual elections, rotation of office, legislative supremacy, and the diffusion of political power through decentralization in order to prevent its consolidation in a few hands.

Although the colonial heritage of particularism, the ideology of the Revolution, and the burgeoning of democratic thought all contributed significantly to the creation of a political persuasion that stressed the importance of local autonomy, it was the actual social and economic conditions under which many people lived during the 1780s that sustained the perspective of localism and made it especially meaningful to a large number of Americans. This is because a very substantial portion of the people at this time were small farmers who lived in simple, isolated, and provincial communities. Since at best they had only a tangential connection with the market economy, it was in the interest of these people to want a weak, inactive, and frugal government which would require few taxes and for the most part leave them alone, and for them to believe that whatever government was necessary should be kept as close to home as possible. It was in these marginally commercial or agrarian areas that the fear of a remote central government was greatest, and that the proponents of democracy and the constitutional concept of states' rights found their firmest supporters.

Ambiguous State-Federal Provisions

It does not follow from this that everyone who supported the philosophy of states' rights underlying the Articles of Confederation was necessarily an agrarian or a democrat. New Englanders and Southerners, who felt secure about being able to control the democratic impulses unleashed by the Revolution in their home states but who distrusted each other and who disliked each other's life styles, also supported the adoption of the Articles of Confederation rather than enter into a strong national government where they might be subject to each other's influence. Others undoubtedly favored local rule simply because it was where they had power and not because it was where the popular will could best be expressed. And still others, although fearful and critical of democracy, believed republicanism could only operate in a small and homogeneous area. But as the 1780s developed and the state governments tended to be susceptible to democratic and popular pressures, many people began to change their minds and rethink and even restructure the ideology of the Revolution. To a very considerable extent it was the concern over the vulnerability of the state governments to popular control and to what was viewed as the vices of the people that was at the heart of the movement for the creation of a strong national government. No doubt the struggle over the adoption of the Constitution was a very complicated one, but once overriding political considerations and local and particularistic interests are accounted for, the most basic division appears to have been between cosmopolitan, commercial, and elite-minded Americans on the one hand, and provincial, agrarian, and democratic Americans on the other.

By creating a national government with the authority to act directly upon individuals, by denying to the states many of the prerogatives that they formerly had, and by leaving open to the central government the possibility of claiming for itself many powers not explicitly assigned to it, the Constitution and Bill of Rights as finally ratified substantially increased the strength of the central government at the expense of the states. But the Constitution did not make the states clearly subservient to the federal government. It did not, for example, provide as James Madison and others wanted, for the central government to have a formal negative on all state laws. In fact, the framers of the Constitution in Philadelphia in 1787 were fearful that if they went too far in reducing the power of the states the Constitution would not be ratified. Consequently, many of the provisions dealing with state-federal relations were ambiguous, and in the debate over ratification the Constitution's supporters went out of their way to emphasize the federal nature of the newly created government. Further, by failing to provide for an ultimate arbiter to interpret the Constitution, the new frame of government became open to the logical, although controversial, interpretation that this power rightly belonged to the states. Although most states' rights advocates in the late eighteenth century would have much preferred the kind of central government provided for in the Articles of Confederation, they could nonetheless continue to argue their position under the Constitution by using the Tenth Amendment to claim that the powers granted to the new government should be strictly interpreted.

Varying States' Rights Arguments

The political discord that developed on the national level during the early 1790s did not correspond to the divisions that had taken place over the adoption of the United States Constitution. Although in opposing Alexander Hamilton's financial program,[1] Thomas Jefferson and James Madison made some appeal to the need for a strict interpretation of the Constitution, they were not thinking in the agrarian and democratic terms of the Antifederalists. Only after John Adams led the country into an undeclared naval war with France[2] and Hamilton and his supporters, with the initial cooperation of Adams, passed the Alien and Sedition Acts[3] and began to place the country on a war footing did Jefferson and Madison adopt an extreme states' rights position with the Kentucky and Virginia Resolutions.[4]

There were both similarities and differences between the way the Republicans used the states' rights argument in the Kentucky and Virginia Resolutions and the way the Antifederalists had used it. Since the Kentucky and Virginia Resolutions were above all else a political platform, a rallying call for support to overthrow the Federalists in the election of 1800, it was grounded in the same majoritarian sentiment that had made the Antifederalist persuasion attractive to so many advocates. But by formulating their states' rights position in terms of a legal procedure or "rightful remedy" by which the states could "interpose" or "nullify" an act of Congress, and by formulating the compact theory of the Constitution in such a way that it could be used (as it eventually was by a later generation) to argue the unqualified sovereignty of the states and their right to withdraw from the Union, Jefferson and Madison added new elements to the states' rights argument.

1. Alexander Hamilton, first secretary of the treasury, believed a strong currency and public investment would uphold the nation. He supported a strong federal government.

2. John Adams built up the nation's naval defenses in the midst of maritime disputes with France, which had raided numerous American ships.

3. The Alien and Sedition Acts allowed the president to deport aliens suspected of posing a threat to the government and imposed strict limits on speech that criticized the government.

4. The Kentucky and Virginia Resolutions stated that the federal government was not authorized to exercise powers not specifically delegated to it by the Constitution.

For the proponents of the agrarian and majoritarian Antifederalist persuasion the concept of states' rights was really that part of a vague political philosophy concerned with the correct and safe distribution of power between the states and the federal government; and since the Antifederalists saw the proper kind of central government as having only explicitly defined and limited powers they had not been concerned with the problem of how to "correctly interpret" a federal constitution. Nor had the Antifederalists, for all their particularism, ever doubted the need, value, and permanency of some kind of central government and did not think in terms that even implied a right of secession. Most Antifederalists were in total agreement with the assertion in the Articles of Confederation "that the Union shall be perpetual."

Weakening States' Rights

Once in power, much to the chagrin of Antifederalist types and states' rights advocates, Jefferson and Madison during the period of their extended ascendancy, 1800–1817, did little to advance the cause of states' rights and much to weaken it. Jefferson, for example, refused to countenance any amendments to the United States Constitution that would formally weaken the federal government, and while he went along with the removal of a number of Federalist judges from office he did not lead an assault upon the authority of the national judiciary. On the other hand, Jefferson expanded the powers of the national government through the purchase of Louisiana and the adoption and enforcement of his controversial embargo policy.[5] Madison was even more of a nationalist than his predecessor. In 1809 he called out troops to uphold the authority of the United States Supreme Court in *United States v. Peters* when the governor of Pennsylvania tried to use the state militia to resist the decision. In 1811, over even Jefferson's objections, he appointed Joseph Story, an extreme nationalist, to

5. Thomas Jefferson's embargo policy, aimed at Britain and France due to tensions with both countries, forbade international trade by U.S. merchants.

the High Court. And in 1816 he requested and signed into law the bill creating the Second Bank of the United States and called for an amendment to the United States Constitution to authorize a federal program of internal improvements.

Despite this neither Jefferson nor Madison repudiated the states' rights position their party had adopted in 1798, and for many, probably even a majority of the Democratic-Republicans it remained the true and unfulfilled credo of the party. This is important because as the unsuccessful opponents of the Constitution the Antifederalists and their ideas were viewed as suspect and even seditious during the 1790s. On the other hand the Democratic-Republican victory in 1800 legitimized the principles of the Kentucky and Virginia Resolutions and allowed countless Americans, including Andrew Jackson and John C. Calhoun, who during the 1820s and 1830s were to call for a rebirth of the "principles of '98," to claim they were the true heirs of Jeffersonian principles.

When the Federalists adopted the states' rights argument in the early nineteenth century it was for a purpose essentially antithetical to the one for which it had been used up to that time. For it was clear that the Federalists had more and more hopelessly become a minority party, and that they were using the states' rights argument in a deliberately obstructionist fashion. The Federalists, in opposing the Louisiana Purchase and Jefferson's embargo and the policies of the national government during the War of 1812, tried to use the demand for a narrow interpretation of the Constitution and the states' rights argument as a way to thwart rather than fulfill the idea of majority rule. Moreover, in the course of their opposition to Republican policies, Federalist spokesmen asserted not simply the right of the states to judge the validity of acts of Congress, but also frequently discussed and even espoused disunion. The Federalists after 1800 thus laid bare, in a way the Republicans had not, the disunionist tendencies that might, but also did not have to, be extrapolated from the states' rights argument. It matters not that most of these statements were blustering threats rather than actual plans or that a much more moderate point of view was adopted by the Hartford Convention.[6] In the eyes of most Americans the Federalist party was forever to be considered the party of treason, and its blatant reversal from its nationalist position of the 1790s was viewed as an opportunistic act brought about by a need to protect its interests rather than from any commitment to political and constitutional principles.

Resurgence of States' Rights Arguments

Following the end of the War of 1812 the country was swept by a spirit of intense nationalism, and while there were occasional attempts to make use of the states' rights argument to oppose it, they were not very effective. This postwar nationalism, tied as it was to a period of prosperity and sweeping economic growth, came to an abrupt end in 1819, however, when the country underwent its first national depression. The reaction was enormous, and there followed a decade of intense political strife and a tremendous resurgence of agrarian, democratic, and states' rights thought.

Because of the dramatic shift that took place in the thinking of many of its leading statesmen and because of the elaborate and definite procedure that John C. Calhoun provided for state action, what occurred in South Carolina has received so much attention from historians that it has distorted the real significance of the widespread reemergence of states' rights thought in the 1820s. The fact is its development in South Carolina during the 1820s simply was not typical of how the states' rights argument was being used in most other parts, north and south, of the country.

More pervasive and important for giving tone and direction to the 1820s was the opposition to a federal program of internal improvements and the reaction to the numerous na-

6. The Hartford Convention (1814–1815) was a secret meeting of Federalists who opposed Jeffersonian-Republican policies and the War of 1812. They proposed a larger convention to revise the Constitution.

tionalist decisions that the Supreme Court under John Marshall's leadership had been handing down since 1810. The main source of the hostility to the High Court is to be found in the reemergence, after 1819, of an extreme democratic and agrarian rhetoric which brought with it a deep hostility to the numerous market-oriented enterprises, particularly banks, corporations, creditors, and absentee landholders whose interests the Supreme Court had generally defended from attack by various states. Closely related to this was the growth, especially on the local level during the 1820s, of demands to make the state governments more immediately and directly responsible to the will of the people. This included demands for an increase in the number of elective officers, a further expansion of the suffrage, a more proportionate form of representation, ways of making judges more responsive to popular sentiment, and a general desire for the weakening of the national government's power. Of course, not all supporters of the states' rights doctrine in the 1820s were necessarily advocates of agrarianism or democracy. John C. Calhoun . . . did not support either concept, while neither John Taylor nor Spencer Roane of Virginia was terribly interested in democratic reform on the local level. But these were mainly exceptions, very significant exceptions to be sure, but still exceptions, for the main thrust of states' rights thought in the 1820s was in the agrarian and democratic direction that culminated in Andrew Jackson's election to the presidency in 1828.

The Bill of Rights

CHAPTER 2

Supreme Court Interpretations of the Tenth Amendment

The Tenth Amendment Does Not Entitle States to Reject Federal Institutions

John Marshall

The states' rights debates in the decades following the Constitution's ratification did not take place solely in the executive and legislative branches of American government. The judicial branch played a role as well when cases concerning the state-federal relationship came before the Supreme Court.

One important early case was that of McCulloch v. Maryland *(1819). James McCulloch, an employee of the federal Bank of the United States, refused to pay taxes imposed by the state of Maryland on the bank. McCulloch contended that a state's taxing of the national bank was an improper interference in federal operations. Maryland argued that the formation of a national bank was not a power bestowed to the federal government by the Constitution and that prohibiting the power of a state to tax was a violation of states' rights.*

The Court unanimously decided in favor of McCulloch, declaring that Congress did have the power to create a national bank and that the states did not have the power to tax a federal institution. In writing the opinion of the Court, which is excerpted here, Chief Justice John Marshall conceded that the Constitution did not explicitly authorize Congress to establish a national bank. However, he insisted that the wording of the Tenth Amendment gave the government implied powers. The creation of a national bank was consistent with the Constitution's goal of providing for the general welfare of the people, he concluded.

The McCulloch v. Maryland *decision was a landmark case because it validated the idea that the federal government possessed implied powers through its execution of regular govern-*

John Marshall, *McCulloch v. Maryland*, 1819.

mental operations. It also established boundaries in the division of state and federal powers by asserting that the states cannot tax the federal government.

John Marshall was a lawyer, special envoy to Paris, Federalist congressman, and secretary of state before being appointed chief justice of the Supreme Court by President John Adams. He served in that position from 1801 to 1835 and set a precedent establishing the Court as the final judge in state-federal disputes. He also underscored the Court's role as interpreter of the Constitution.

In the case to be determined, the defendant, a sovereign State [Maryland], denies the obligation of a law enacted by the legislature of the Union, and the plaintiff, on his part, contests the validity of an act which has been passed by the legislature of that State. The constitution of our country, in its most interesting and vital parts, is to be considered; the conflicting powers of the government of the Union and of its members, as marked in that constitution, are to be discussed; and an opinion given, which may essentially influence the great operations of the government. No tribunal can approach such a question without a deep sense of its importance, and of the awful responsibility involved in its decision. But it must be decided peacefully, or remain a source of hostile legislation, perhaps of hostility of a still more serious nature; and if it is to be so decided, by this tribunal alone can the decision be made. On the Supreme Court of the United States has the constitution of our country devolved this important duty.

The first question made in the cause is, has Congress power to incorporate a bank?. . .

In discussing this question, the counsel for the State of Maryland have deemed it of some importance, in the construction of the constitution, to consider that instrument not as emanating from the people, but as the act of sovereign and independent States. The powers of the general government, it has been said, are delegated by the States, who alone are truly sovereign; and must be exercised in subordination to the States, who alone possess supreme dominion.

Government Proceeds from the People

It would be difficult to sustain this proposition. The Convention which framed the constitution was indeed elected by the State legislatures. But the instrument, when it came from their hands, was a mere proposal, without obligation, or pretensions to it. It was reported to the then existing Congress of the United States, with a request that it might "be submitted to a convention of delegates, chosen in each State by the people thereof, under the recommendation of its legislature, for their assent and ratification." This mode of proceeding was adopted; and by the convention, by Congress, and by the State legislatures, the instrument was submitted to the people. They acted upon it in the only manner in which they can act safely, effectively, and wisely, on such a subject, by assembling in convention. It is true, they assembled in their several States— and where else should they have assembled? No political dreamer was ever wild enough to think of breaking down the lines which separate the States, and of compounding the American people into one common mass. Of consequence, when they act, they act in their States. But the measures they adopt do not, on that account, cease to be the measures of the people themselves, or become the measures of the State governments.

From these conventions the constitution derives its whole authority. The government proceeds directly from the people; is "ordained and established" in the name of the people; and is declared to be ordained, "in order to form a more perfect union, establish justice, ensure domestic tranquility, and secure the blessings of liberty to themselves and to their posterity." The assent of the States, in their sovereign capacity, is implied in calling a convention, and thus submitting that instrument to the people. But the people were at perfect liberty to accept or reject it; and their act was final. It required not the affirmance, and could not be negatived, by the State governments. The constitution, when thus adopted, was of complete obligation, and bound the State sovereignties. . . .

[It], is, emphatically, and truly, a government of the people. In form and in substance it emanates from them. Its powers are granted by them, and are to be exercised directly on them, and for their benefit.

Enumerated Powers

This government is acknowledged by all to be one of enumerated powers. The principle, that it can exercise only the powers granted to it, [is] now universally admitted. But the question respecting the extent of the powers actually granted, is perpetually arising, and will probably continue to arise, as long as our system shall exist. . . .

Among the enumerated powers, we do not find that of establishing a bank or creating a corporation. But there is no phrase in the instrument which, like the articles of confederation, excludes incidental or implied powers; and which requires that everything granted shall be expressly and minutely described. Even the 10th amendment, which was framed for the purpose of quieting the excessive jealousies which had been excited, omits the word "expressly," and declares only that the powers "not delegated to the United States, nor prohibited to the States, are reserved to the States or to the people"; thus leaving the question, whether the particular power which may become the subject of contest has been delegated to the one government, or prohibited to the other, to depend on a fair construction of the whole instrument. The men who drew and adopted this amendment had experienced the embarrassments resulting from the insertion of this word in the articles of confederation, and probably omitted it to avoid those embarrassments. A constitution, to contain an accurate detail of all the subdivisions of which its great powers will admit, and of all the means by which they may be carried into execution, would partake of the prolixity of a legal code, and could scarcely be embraced by the human mind. It would probably never be understood by the public. Its nature, therefore, requires, that only its great outlines should be marked, its important objects designated, and the minor ingredients which compose those objects be deduced from the nature of the objects themselves. That this idea was entertained by the framers of the American constitution, is not only to be inferred from the nature of the instrument, but from the language. Why else were some of the limitations, found in the ninth section of the 1st article, introduced? It is also, in some degree, warranted by their having omitted to use any restrictive term which might prevent its receiving a fair and just interpretation. In considering this question, then, we must never forget that it is a constitution we are expounding. . . .

The Meaning of "Necessary"

But the constitution of the United States has not left the right of Congress to employ the necessary means, for the execution of the powers conferred on the government, to general reasoning. To its enumeration of powers is added that of making "all laws which shall be necessary and proper for carrying into execution the foregoing powers, and all other powers vested by this constitution, in the government of the United States, or in any department thereof."

The counsel for the State of Maryland have urged various arguments, to prove that this clause, though in terms a grant of power, is not so in effect; but is really restrictive of the general right, which might otherwise be implied, of selecting means for executing the enumerated powers. . . .

Almost all compositions contain words, which, taken in their rigorous sense, would convey a meaning different from that which is obviously intended. It is essential to just construction, that many words which import something excessive should be understood in a more mitigated sense—in that sense which common usage justifies. The word "necessary" is of this description. It has not a fixed character peculiar to itself. It admits of all degrees of comparison; and is often connected with other words, which increase or diminish the impression the mind receives of the urgency it imports. A thing may be necessary, very necessary, absolutely or indispensably necessary. To no mind would the same idea be conveyed by these several phrases. This comment on the word is well illustrated by the passage cited at the bar, from the 20th section of the 1st article of the constitution. It is, we think, impossible to compare the sentence which prohibits a State from laying "imposts, or duties on imports or exports, except what may be absolutely necessary for executing its inspection laws," with that which authorizes Congress "to make all laws which shall be necessary and proper for carrying into execution" the powers of the general government, without feeling a conviction that the convention understood itself to change materially the meaning of the word "necessary," by prefixing the word "absolutely." This word, then, like others, is used in various senses; and, in its construction, the subject, the context, the intention of the person using them, are all to be taken into view.

Executing Powers for the Nation's Benefit

Let this be done in the case under consideration. The subject is the execution of those great powers on which the welfare of a nation essentially depends. It must have been the intention of those who gave these powers, to insure, as far as human prudence could insure, their beneficial execution. This could not be done by confiding the choice of means to such narrow limits as not to leave it in the power of Congress to adopt any which might be appropriate, and which were conducive to the end. This provision is made in a constitution intended to endure for ages to come, and, consequently, to be adapted to the various crises of human affairs. To have prescribed the means by which government should, in all future time, execute its powers, would have been to change, entirely, the character of the instrument, and give it the properties of a legal code. It would have been an unwise attempt to provide, by immutable rules, for exigencies which, if foreseen at all, must have been seen dimly, and which can be best provided for as they occur. To have declared that the best means shall not be used, but those alone without which the power given would be nugatory, would have been to deprive the legislature of the capacity to avail itself of experience, to exercise its reason, and to accommodate its legislation to circumstances. If we apply this principle of construction to any of the powers of the government, we shall find it so pernicious in its operation that we shall be compelled to discard it. . . .

The result of the most careful and attentive consideration bestowed upon this clause is, that if it does not enlarge, it cannot be construed to restrain the powers of Congress, or to impair the rights of the legislature to exercise its best judgment in the selection of measures to carry into execution the constitutional powers of the government. If no other motive for its insertion can be suggested, a sufficient one is found in the desire to remove all doubts respecting the right to legislate on that vast mass of incidental powers which must be involved in the constitution, if that instrument be not a splendid bauble.

We admit, as all must admit, that the powers of the government are limited, and that its limits are not to be transcended. But we think the sound construction of the constitution must allow to the national legislature that discretion, with respect to the means by which the powers it confers are to be carried into execution, which will enable that body to perform the high duties assigned to it, in the manner most beneficial to the people. Let the end be legitimate, let it be within the scope of the constitution, and all means which are appropriate, which are plainly adapted to that end, which are not prohibited, but consist with the letter and spirit of the constitution, are constitutional. . . .

A National Bank Is Constitutional

Should Congress, in the execution of its powers, adopt measures which are prohibited by the constitution; or should Congress, under the pretext of executing its powers, pass laws for the accomplishment of objects not entrusted to the government; it would become the painful duty of this tribunal, should a case requiring such a decision come before it, to say that such an act was not the law of the land. But where the law is not prohibited, and is really calculated to effect any of the objects entrusted to the government, to undertake here to inquire into the degree of its necessity, would be to pass the line which circumscribes the judicial department, and to tread on legislative ground. This court disclaims all pretensions to such a power.

After this declaration, it can scarcely be necessary to say that the existence of State banks can have no possible influence on the question. No trace is to be found in the constitution of an intention to create a dependence of the government of the Union on those of the States, for the execution of the great powers assigned to it. Its means are adequate to its ends; and on those means alone was it expected to rely for the accomplishment of its ends. To impose on it the necessity of resorting to means which it cannot control, which another government may furnish or withhold, would render its course precarious, the result of its measures uncertain, and create a dependence on other governments, which might disappoint its most important designs, and is incompatible with the language of the constitution. But were it otherwise, the choice of means implies a right to choose a national bank in preference to State banks, and Congress alone can make the election.

After the most deliberate consideration, it is the unanimous and decided opinion of this Court, that the act to incorporate the Bank of the United States is a law made in pursuance of the constitution, and is a part of the supreme law of the land. . . .

It being the opinion of the Court, that the act incorporating the bank is constitutional; and that the power of establishing a branch in the State of Maryland might be properly exercised by the bank itself, we proceed to inquire—

. . .Whether the State of Maryland may, without violating the constitution, tax that branch?. . .

State Taxation

The sovereignty of a State extends to everything which exists by its own authority, or is so introduced by its permission; but does it extend to those means which are employed by Congress to carry into execution powers conferred on that body by the people of the United States? We think it demonstrable that it does not. Those powers are not given by the people of a single State. They are given by the people of the United States, to a government whose laws, made in pursuance of the constitution, are declared to be supreme. Consequently, the people of a single State cannot confer a sovereignty which will extend over them.

If we measure the power of taxation residing in a State, by the extent of sovereignty which the people of a single State possess, and can confer on its government, we have an intelligible standard, applicable to every case to which the power may be applied. We have a principle which leaves the power of taxing the people and property of a State unimpaired; which leaves to a State the command of all its resources, and which places beyond its reach, all those powers which are conferred by the people of the United States on the government of the Union, and all those means which are given for the purpose of carrying those powers into execution. We have a principle which is safe for the States, and safe for the Union. We are relieved, as we ought to be, from clashing sovereignty; from interfering powers; from a repugnancy between a right in one government to pull down what there is an acknowledged right in another to build up; from the incompatibility of a right in one government to destroy what there is a right in another to preserve. We are not driven to the perplexing inquiry, so unfit for the judicial department, what degree of taxation is the legitimate use, and what degree may amount to the abuse of the power. The attempt to use it on the means employed by the government of the Union, in pursuance of the constitution, is itself an abuse, because it is the usurpation of a power which the people of a single State cannot give.

We find, then, on just theory, a total failure of this original right to tax the means employed by the government of the Union, for the execution of its powers. The right never existed, and the question whether it has been surrendered, cannot arise.

But, waiving this theory for the present, let us resume the inquiry, whether this power can be exercised by the respective States, consistently with a fair construction of the constitution?

The National Legislature Can Be Trusted

That the power to tax involves the power to destroy that the power to destroy may defeat and render useless the power to create; that there is a plain repugnance, in conferring on one government a power to control the constitutional measures of another, which other, with respect to those very measures, is declared to be supreme over that which exerts the control, are propositions not to be denied. But all inconsistencies are to be reconciled by the magic of the word CONFIDENCE. Taxation, it is said, does not necessarily and unavoidably destroy. To carry it to the excess of destruction would be an abuse, to presume which, would banish that confidence which is essential to all government.

But is this a case of confidence? Would the people of any one State trust those of another with a power to control the most insignificant operations of their State government? We know they would not. Why, then, should we suppose that the people of any one State should be willing to trust those of another with a power to control the operations of a government to which they have confided their most important and most valuable interests? In the legislature of the Union alone, are all represented. The legislature of the Union alone, therefore, can be trusted by the people with the power of controlling measures which concern all, in the confidence that it will not be abused. This, then, is not a case of confidence, and we must consider it as it really is.

If we apply the principle for which the State of Maryland contends, to the constitution generally, we shall find it capable of changing totally the character of that instrument. We shall find it capable of arresting all the measures of the government, and of prostrating it at the foot of the States. The American people have declared their constitution, and the laws made in pursuance thereof, to be supreme; but this principle would transfer the supremacy, in fact, to the States.

If the States may tax one instrument, employed by the government in the execution of its powers, they may tax any and every other instrument. They may tax the mail; they may tax the mint; they may tax patent rights; they may tax the papers of the custom-house; they may tax judicial process; they may tax all the means employed by the government, to an excess which would defeat all the ends of government. This was not intended by the American people. They did not design to make their government dependent on the States. . . .

States Cannot Interfere with Federal Laws

The Court has bestowed on this subject its most deliberate consideration. The result is a conviction that the States have no power, by taxation or otherwise, to retard, impede, burden, or in any manner control, the operations of the constitutional laws enacted by Congress to carry into execution the powers vested in the general government. This is, we think, the unavoidable consequence of that supremacy which the constitution has declared.

We are unanimously of opinion, that the law passed by the legislature of Maryland, imposing a tax on the Bank of the United States, is unconstitutional and void.

This opinion does not deprive the States of any resources which they originally possessed. It does not extend to a tax paid by the real property of the bank, in common with the other real property within the State, nor to a tax imposed on the interest which the citizens of Maryland may hold in this institution, in common with other property of the same description throughout the State. But this is a tax on the operations of the bank, and is, consequently, a tax on the operation of an instrument employed by the government of the Union to carry its powers into execution. Such a tax must be unconstitutional.

The Tenth Amendment Limits the Authority of Congress

William Rufus Day

By the mid-nineteenth century, the states' rights debate erupted into increased sectionalism, secession, and eventually the Civil War. During this time, the issue moved beyond the Supreme Court and pervaded American society. The post–Civil War era was a time of healing the Union, and fewer court cases centered specifically on the state-federal relationship. By the early twentieth century, however, states' rights debates resumed as the federal government expanded its reach by promoting laws based on humanitarian social movements.

In 1918 Hammer v. Dagenhart *came before the Supreme Court and challenged the constitutionality of the Keating-Owen Act (1916). The act, based on a social movement seeking to end child labor, aimed to exclude from interstate commerce all goods produced by factories and mines that employed children. In the court case, U.S. district attorney W.C. Hammer claimed that Ronald Dagenhart was in violation of the Keating-Owen Act because he allowed his two teenaged sons to work in a mill.*

The Supreme Court ruled 5-4 against Hammer and held that the Keating-Owen Act was unconstitutional. In the opinion of the Court excerpted below, Justice William Rufus Day concedes that Congress has the power to regulate interstate commerce. However, says Day, the Keating-Owen Act goes beyond controlling commerce between states; it regulates the manner in which goods are produced within states. Therefore, it violates the Tenth Amendment. Day concludes that child labor should fall under state, not federal, jurisdiction. Hammer v. Dagenhart *thus placed obstacles before the federal government's ability to legislate child labor.*

William Rufus Day, *Hammer v. Dagenhart*, June 3, 1918.

William Rufus Day was an associate justice of the Supreme Court from 1903 to 1922. Prior to his Supreme Court appointment by President Theodore Roosevelt, Day served as secretary of state under President William McKinley and then as chairman of the peace settlement commission after the Spanish-American War (1898).

A bill was filed in the United States District Court for the Western District of North Carolina by a father in his own behalf and as next friend of his two minor sons, one under the age of fourteen years and the other between the ages of fourteen and sixteen years, employees in a cotton mill at Charlotte, North Carolina, to enjoin the enforcement of the act of Congress intended to prevent interstate commerce in the products of child labor. Act of Sept. 1, 1916, c. 432, 39 Stat. 675.

Power to Prohibit?

The District Court held the act unconstitutional and entered a decree enjoining its enforcement. This appeal brings the case here. . . .

The attack upon the act rests upon three propositions: first: it is not a regulation of interstate and foreign commerce; second: it contravenes the Tenth Amendment to the Constitution; third: it conflicts with the Fifth Amendment to the Constitution.

The controlling question for decision is: is it within the authority of Congress in regulating commerce among the States to prohibit the transportation in interstate commerce of manufactured goods, the product of a factory in which, within thirty days prior to their removal therefrom, children under the age of fourteen have been employed or permitted to work, or children between the ages of fourteen and sixteen years have been employed or permitted to work more than eight hours in any day, or more than six days in any week, or after the hour of seven o'clock P.M. or before the hour of 6 o'clock A.M.?

The power essential to the passage of this act, the Government contends, is found in the commerce clause of the Constitution, which authorizes Congress to regulate commerce with foreign nations and among the States.

In *Gibbons v. Ogden* [1824], Chief Justice [John] Marshall, speaking for this court and defining the extent and nature of the commerce power, said, "It is the power to regulate; that is, to prescribe the rule by which commerce is to be governed." In other words, the power is one to control the means by which commerce is carried on, which is directly the contrary of the assumed right to forbid commerce from moving, and thus destroy it as to particular commodities. But it is insisted that adjudged cases in this court establish the doctrine that the power to regulate given to Congress incidentally includes the authority to prohibit the movement of ordinary commodities, and therefore that the subject is not open for discussion. The cases demonstrate the contrary. They rest upon the character of the particular subjects dealt with, and the fact that the scope of governmental authority, state or national, possessed over them is such that the authority to prohibit is as to them but the exertion of the power to regulate.

Past Opinions on Commerce Regulation

The first of these cases is *Champion v. Ames* [1903], the so-called *Lottery Case*, in which it was held that Congress might pass a law having the effect to keep the channels of commerce free from use in the transportation of tickets used in the promotion of lottery schemes. In *Hipolite Egg Co. v. United States* [1911], this court sustained the power of Congress to pass the Pure Food and Drug Act, which prohibited the introduction into the States by means of interstate commerce of impure foods and drugs. In *Hoke v. United States* [1913], this court sustained the constitutionality of the so-called "White Slave Traffic Act," whereby the transportation of a woman in interstate commerce for the purpose of prostitution was forbidden.

In that case, we said, having reference to the authority of Congress, under the regulatory power, to protect the channels of interstate commerce:

> If the facility of interstate transportation can be taken away from the demoralization of lotteries, the debasement of obscene literature, the contagion of diseased cattle or persons, the impurity of food and drugs, the like facility can be taken away from the systematic enticement to and the enslavement in prostitution and debauchery of women, and, more insistently, of girls.

In *Caminetti v. United States* [1917], we held that Congress might prohibit the transportation of women in interstate commerce for the purposes of debauchery and kindred purposes. In *Clark Distilling Co. v. Western Maryland Ry. Co.*, [1917] the power of Congress over the transportation of intoxicating liquors was sustained. In the course of the opinion, it was said:

> The power conferred is to regulate, and the very terms of the grant would seem to repel the contention that only prohibition of movement in interstate commerce was embraced. And the cogency of this is manifest, since, if the doctrine were applied to those manifold and important subjects of interstate commerce as to which Congress from the beginning has regulated, not prohibited, the existence of government under the Constitution would be no longer possible.

And, concluding the discussion which sustained the authority of the Government to prohibit the transportation of liquor in interstate commerce, the court said:

> ... the exceptional nature of the subject here regulated is the basis upon which the exceptional power exerted must rest, and affords no ground for any fear that such power may be constitutionally extended to things which it may not, consistently with the guarantees of the Constitution, embrace.

Defining Commerce

In each of these instances, the use of interstate transportation was necessary to the accomplishment of harmful results. In other words, although the power over interstate transportation was to regulate, that could only be accomplished by prohibiting the use of the facilities of interstate commerce to effect the evil intended.

This element is wanting in the present case. The thing intended to be accomplished by this statute is the denial of the facilities of interstate commerce to those manufacturers in the States who employ children within the prohibited ages. The act, in its effect, does not regulate transportation among the States, but aims to standardize the ages at which children may be employed in mining and manufacturing within the States. The goods shipped are, of themselves, harmless. The act permits them to be freely shipped after thirty days from the time of their removal from the factory. When offered for shipment, and before transportation begins, the labor of their production is over, and the mere fact that they were intended for interstate commerce transportation does not make their production subject to federal control under the commerce power.

Commerce

consists of intercourse and traffic, and includes the transportation of persons and property, as well as the purchase, sale and exchange of commodities.

The making of goods and the mining of coal are not commerce, nor does the fact that these things are to be afterwards shipped or used in interstate commerce make their production a part thereof.

Over interstate transportation or its incidents, the regulatory power of Congress is ample, but the production of articles intended for interstate commerce is a matter of local regulation.

When the commerce begins is determined not by the character of the commodity, nor by the intention of the owner to transfer it to another state for sale, nor by his preparation of it for transportation, but by its actual delivery to a common carrier for transportation, or the actual commencement of its transfer to another state. (Mr. Justice Jackson in *In re Green* [1890].)

This principle has been recognized often in this court. If it were otherwise, all manufacture intended for interstate shipment would be brought under federal control to the practical exclusion of the authority of the States, a result certainly not contemplated by the framers of the Constitution when they vested in Congress the authority to regulate commerce among the States.

Limits of Congressional Power

It is further contended that the authority of Congress may be exerted to control interstate commerce in the shipment of child-made goods because of the effect of the circulation of such goods in other States where the evil of this class of labor has been recognized by local legislation, and the right to thus employ child labor has been more rigorously restrained than in the State of production. In other words, that the unfair competition thus engendered may be controlled by closing the channels of interstate commerce to manufacturers in those States where the local laws do not meet what Congress deems to be the more just standard of other States.

There is no power vested in Congress to require the States to exercise their police power so as to prevent possible unfair competition. Many causes may cooperate to give one State, by reason of local laws or conditions, an economic advantage over others. The Commerce Clause was not intended to give to Congress a general authority to equalize such conditions. In some of the States, laws have been passed fixing minimum wages for women, in others, the local law regulates the hours of labor of women in various employments. Business done in such States may be at an economic disadvantage when compared with States which have no such regulations; surely, this fact does not give Congress the power to deny transportation in interstate commerce to those who carry on business where the hours of labor and the rate of compensation for women have not been fixed by a standard in use in other States and approved by Congress.

The grant of power to Congress over the subject of interstate commerce was to enable it to regulate such commerce, and not to give it authority to control the States in their exercise of the police power over local trade and manufacture.

Upholding States' Rights

The grant of authority over a purely federal matter was not intended to destroy the local power always existing and carefully reserved to the States in the Tenth Amendment to the Constitution.

Police regulations relating to the internal trade and affairs of the States have been uniformly recognized as within such control. "This," said this court in *United States v. Dewitt* [1869],

> has been so frequently declared by this court, results so obviously from the terms of the Constitution, and has been so fully explained and supported on former occasions that we think it unnecessary to enter again upon the discussion. . . .

In the judgment [*Gibbons v. Ogden*] which established the broad power of Congress over interstate commerce, Chief Justice Marshall said:

> They [inspection laws] act upon the subject before it becomes an article of foreign commerce, or of commerce among the states, and prepare it for that purpose. They form a portion of that immense mass of legislation which

embraces everything within the territory of a state not surrendered to the general government, all which can be most advantageously exercised by the states themselves. Inspection laws, quarantine laws, health laws of every description, as well as laws for regulating the internal commerce of a state and those which respect turnpike roads, ferries, etc., are component parts of this mass.

And in *Dartmouth College v. Woodward* [1819], the same great judge said:

That the framers of the constitution did not intend to restrain the states in the regulation of their civil institutions, adopted for internal government, and that the instrument they have given us is not to be so construed may be admitted.

That there should be limitations upon the right to employ children in mines and factories in the interest of their own and the public welfare, all will admit. That such employment is generally deemed to require regulation is shown by the fact that the brief of counsel states that every State in the Union has a law upon the subject, limiting the right to thus employ children. In North Carolina, the State wherein is located the factory in which the employment was had in the present case, no child under twelve years of age is permitted to work.

It may be desirable that such laws be uniform, but our Federal Government is one of enumerated powers; "this principle," declared Chief Justice Marshall in *McCulloch v. Maryland* [1819], "is universally admitted."

A statute must be judged by its natural and reasonable effect. The control by Congress over interstate commerce cannot authorize the exercise of authority not entrusted to it by the Constitution. The maintenance of the authority of the States over matters purely local is as essential to the preservation of our institutions, as is the conservation of the supremacy of the federal power in all matters entrusted to the Nation by the Federal Constitution.

No Federal Invasion of Local Power

In interpreting the Constitution, it must never be forgotten that the Nation is made up of States to which are entrusted the powers of local government. And to them and to the people the powers not expressly delegated to the National Government are reserved. The power of the States to regulate their purely internal affairs by such laws as seem wise to the local authority is inherent, and has never been surrendered to the general government. To sustain this statute would not be, in our judgment, a recognition of the lawful exertion of congressional authority over interstate commerce, but would sanction an invasion by the federal power of the control of a matter purely local in its character, and over which no authority has been delegated to Congress in conferring the power to regulate commerce among the States.

We have neither authority nor disposition to question the motives of Congress in enacting this legislation. The purposes intended must be attained consistently with constitutional limitations, and not by an invasion of the powers of the States. This court has no more important function than that which devolves upon it the obligation to preserve inviolate the constitutional limitations upon the exercise of authority, federal and state, to the end that each may continue to discharge, harmoniously with the other, the duties entrusted to it by the Constitution.

In our view, the necessary effect of this act is, by means of a prohibition against the movement in interstate commerce of ordinary commercial commodities, to regulate the hours of labor of children in factories and mines within the States, a purely state authority. Thus, the act in a two-fold sense is repugnant to the Constitution. It not only transcends the authority delegated to Congress over commerce, but also exerts a power as to a purely local matter to which the federal authority does not extend. The far-reaching result of upholding the act cannot be more plainly indicated than by pointing out that, if Congress can thus regulate matters entrusted to local authority by prohibition of the movement of commodities in interstate commerce, all freedom of commerce will be at an end, and the power of the States over local matters may be eliminated, and, thus, our system of government be practically destroyed.

For these reasons, we hold that this law exceeds the constitutional authority of Congress. It follows that the decree of the District Court must be.

Affirmed.

The Tenth Amendment Does Not Deprive the Federal Government of Authority

Harlan Fiske Stone

In the years following Hammer v. Dagenhart *(1918), Supreme Court rulings largely favored states' rights. Then the Great Depression hit in 1929 and lingered through the 1930s. When Franklin Delano Roosevelt was elected president in 1932, he combated the problems of the Depression with the New Deal, a series of federal economic relief and social welfare programs. This legislation increased the responsibilities and scope of the central government because the funding and guidance for these programs came from the federal government rather than state governments.*

United States v. Darby *concerned the final piece of New Deal legislation passed in 1938, the Fair Labor Standards Act (FLSA). The FLSA set maximum hours and minimum wages for workers employed by any industry that shipped goods from state to state. Fred W. Darby, an industrialist from Georgia, was indicted under the FLSA because his employees worked more than the maximum number of hours and were paid less than the minimum wage. Darby challenged the constitutionality of the act, citing the Tenth Amendment. He insisted that because the manufacturing at his lumber company took place within Georgia, the company should be subject to state, not federal, regulation. The Supreme Court disagreed and unanimously upheld the constitutionality of the FLSA.*

In the following excerpt from the Court's opinion, Justice Harlan Fiske Stone explains that the decision overrules a previous precedent-setting decision, Hammer v. Dagenhart *(1918). That decision had concluded that Congress had no authority to*

Harlan Fiske Stone, *United States v. Darby*, February 3, 1941.

regulate labor in states even if the goods produced by that labor were shipped to other states. In Darby, *by contrast, the Court ruled that Congress does have such authority. Stone explains that the Tenth Amendment merely guarantees that powers not granted to the federal government are retained by the states. It does not limit the authority of the federal government to exercise the power granted to it by the Constitution, including the power to regulate commerce.*

Harlan Fiske Stone was dean of Columbia Law School and U.S. attorney general before President Calvin Coolidge appointed him to the Supreme Court in 1925. President Roosevelt made him chief justice in 1941, but he was not in this position at the time of United States v. Darby. *He led the Supreme Court until his death in 1946.*

The two principal questions raised by the record in this case are, first, whether Congress has constitutional power to prohibit the shipment in interstate commerce of lumber manufactured by employees whose wages are less than a prescribed minimum or whose weekly hours of labor at that wage are greater than a prescribed maximum, and, second, whether it has power to prohibit the employment of workmen in the production of goods "for interstate commerce" at other than prescribed wages and hours. A subsidiary question is whether, in connection with such prohibitions, Congress can require the employer subject to them to keep records showing the hours worked each day and week by each of his employees including those engaged "in the production and manufacture of goods, to-wit, lumber, for 'interstate commerce.'"

The Fair Labor Standards Act

Appellee demurred to an indictment found in the district court for southern Georgia charging him with violation of the Fair Labor Standards Act of 1938. The district court sustained the demurrer and quashed the indictment, and the case comes here on direct appeal under § 238 of the Judicial Code as amended, which authorizes an appeal to this Court when the judgment sustaining the demurrer "is based upon the invalidity or construction of the statute upon which the indictment is founded."

The Fair Labor Standards Act set up a comprehensive legislative scheme for preventing the shipment in interstate commerce of certain products and commodities produced in the United States under labor conditions as respects wages and hours which fail to conform to standards set up by the Act. Its purpose, as we judicially know from the declaration of policy in § 2(a) of the Act, and the reports of Congressional committees proposing the legislation, is to exclude from interstate commerce goods produced for the commerce and to prevent their production for interstate commerce under conditions detrimental to the maintenance of the minimum standards of living necessary for health and general wellbeing, and to prevent the use of interstate commerce as the means of competition in the distribution of goods so produced, and as the means of spreading and perpetuating such substandard labor conditions among the workers of the several states. The Act also sets up an administrative procedure whereby those standards may from time to time be modified generally as to industries subject to the Act or within an industry in accordance with specified standards, by an administrator acting in collaboration with "Industry Committees" appointed by him. . . .

Validity of the Act Challenged

The indictment charges that appellee [Darby] is engaged, in the State of Georgia, in the business of acquiring raw materials, which he manufactures into finished lumber with the intent, when manufactured, to ship it in interstate commerce to customers outside the state, and that he does, in fact, so ship a large part of the lumber so produced. There are numerous counts charging appellee with the shipment in interstate commerce from Georgia to points outside the state of lumber in the production of which, for interstate commerce, appellee has employed workmen at less than the prescribed minimum wage or more than the prescribed maximum hours without payment to them of any wage for overtime. Other counts charge the employment by appellee of workmen in the production of lumber for interstate commerce at wages at less than 25 cents an hour or for more than the maximum hours per week without payment to them of the prescribed overtime wage. Still another count charges appellee with failure to keep records showing the hours worked each day a week by each of his employees as required by § 11(c) and the regulation of the administrator, Code of Federal Regulations, and also that appellee unlawfully failed to keep such records of employees engaged "in the production and manufacture of goods, to-wit lumber, for interstate commerce."

The demurrer, so far as now relevant to the appeal, challenged the validity of the Fair Labor Standards Act under the Commerce Clause and the Fifth and Tenth Amendments. The district court quashed the indictment in its entirety upon the broad grounds that the Act, which it interpreted as a regulation of manufacture within the states, is unconstitutional. It declared that manufacture is not interstate commerce, and that the regulation by the Fair Labor Standards Act of wages and hours of employment of those engaged in the manufacture of goods which it is intended at the time of production "may or will be" after production "sold in interstate commerce in part or in whole" is not within the congressional power to regulate interstate commerce.

The effect of the court's decision and judgment is thus to deny the power of Congress to prohibit shipment in interstate commerce of lumber produced for interstate commerce under the proscribed substandard labor conditions of wages and hours, its power to penalize the employer for his failure to conform to the wage and hour provisions in the case of employees engaged in the production of lumber which he intends thereafter to ship in interstate commerce in part or in whole according to the normal course of his business, and its power to compel him to keep records of hours of employment as required by the statute and the regulations of the administrator. . . .

Public Policy and the Present Regulation

The power of Congress over interstate commerce "is complete in itself, may be exercised to its utmost extent, and acknowledges no limitations other than are prescribed in the Constitution." *Gibbons v. Ogden* [1824]. That power can neither be enlarged nor diminished by the exercise or nonexercise of state power. Congress, following its own conception of public policy concerning the restrictions which may appropriately be imposed on interstate commerce, is free to exclude from the commerce articles whose use in the states for which they are destined it may conceive to be injurious to the public health, morals or welfare, even though the state has not sought to regulate their use.

Such regulation is not a forbidden invasion of state power merely because either its motive or its consequence is to restrict the use of articles of commerce within the states of destination, and is not prohibited unless by other Constitutional provisions. It is no objection to the assertion of the power to regulate interstate commerce that its exercise is attended by the same incidents which attend the exercise of the police power of the states.

The motive and purpose of the present regulation are plainly to make effective the Congressional conception of public policy that interstate commerce should not be made the instrument of competition in the distribution of goods produced under substandard labor conditions, which competition is injurious to the commerce and to the states from and to which the commerce flows. The motive and purpose of a regulation of interstate commerce are matters for the legislative judgment upon the exercise of which the Constitution places no restriction, and over which the courts are given no control. "The judicial cannot prescribe to the legislative department of the government limitations upon the exercise of its acknowledged power." *Veazie Bank v. Fenno* [1869]. Whatever their motive and purpose, regulations of commerce which do not infringe some constitutional prohibition are within the plenary power conferred on Congress by the Commerce Clause. Subject only to that limitation, presently to be considered, we conclude that the prohibition of the shipment interstate of goods produced under the forbidden substandard labor conditions is within the constitutional authority of Congress.

Not Following *Hammer v. Dagenhart*

In the more than a century which has elapsed since the decision of *Gibbons v. Ogden*, these principles of constitutional interpretation have been so long and repeatedly recognized by this Court as applicable to the Commerce Clause that there would be little occasion for repeating them now were it not for the decision of this Court twenty-two years ago in *Hammer v. Dagenhart* [1918]. In that case, it was held by a bare majority of the Court, over the powerful and now classic dissent of Mr. Justice [Oliver Wendell] Holmes setting forth the fundamental issues involved, that Congress was without power to exclude the products of child labor from interstate commerce. The reasoning and conclusion of the Court's opinion there cannot be reconciled with the conclusion which we have reached, that the power of Congress under the Commerce Clause is plenary to exclude any article from interstate commerce subject only to the specific prohibitions of the Constitution.

Hammer v. Dagenhart has not been followed. The distinction on which the decision was rested, that Congressional power to prohibit interstate commerce is limited to articles which in themselves have some harmful or deleterious property—a distinction which was novel when made and unsupported by any provision of the Constitution—has long since been abandoned. The thesis of the opinion—that the motive of the prohibition or its effect to control in some measure the use or production within the states of the article thus excluded from the commerce can operate to deprive the regulation of its constitutional authority—has long since ceased to have force. And finally, we have declared

> The authority of the federal government over interstate commerce does not differ in extent or character from that retained by the states over intrastate commerce.

United States v. Rock Royal Cooperative [1939].

The conclusion is inescapable that *Hammer v. Dagenhart* was a departure from the principles which have prevailed in the interpretation of the Commerce Clause both before and since the decision, and that such vitality, as a precedent, as it then had, has long since been exhausted. It should be, and now is, overruled. . . .

Wage and Hour Requirements

Validity of the wage and hour requirements. Section 15(a)(2) and §§ 6 and 7 require employers to conform to the wage and hour provisions with respect to all employees engaged in the production of goods for interstate commerce. As appellee's employees are not alleged to be "engaged in interstate commerce," the validity of the prohibition turns on the question whether the employment, under other than the prescribed labor standards, of employees engaged in the production of goods for interstate commerce is so related to the commerce, and so affects it, as to be within the reach of the power of Congress to regulate it.

To answer this question, we must at the outset determine whether the particular acts charged in the counts which are laid under § 15(a)(2) as they were construed below constitute "production for commerce" within the meaning of the statute. As the Government seeks to apply the statute in the indictment, and as the court below construed the phrase "produced for interstate commerce," it embraces at least the case where an employer engaged, as is appellee, in the manufacture and shipment of goods in filling orders of extrastate customers, manufactures his product with the intent or expectation that, according to the normal course of his business, all or some part of it will be selected for shipment to those customers.

Without attempting to define the precise limits of the phrase, we think the acts alleged in the indictment are within the sweep of the statute. The obvious purpose of the Act was not only to prevent the interstate transportation of the proscribed product, but to stop the initial step toward transportation, production with the purpose of so transporting it. Congress was not unaware that most manufacturing businesses shipping their product in interstate commerce make it in their shops without reference to its ultimate destination, and then, after manufacture, select some of it for shipment interstate and some intrastate, according to the daily demands of their business, and that it would be practically impossible, without disrupting manufacturing businesses, to restrict the prohibited kind of production to the particular pieces of lumber, cloth, furniture or the like which later move in interstate, rather than intrastate, commerce.

The recognized need of drafting a workable statute and the well known circumstances in which it was to be applied are persuasive of the conclusion, which the legislative history supports, that the "production for commerce" intended includes at least production of goods which, at the time of production, the employer, according to the normal course of his business, intends or expects to move in interstate commerce although, through the exigencies of the business, all of the goods may not thereafter actually enter interstate commerce.

Extent of Interstate Commerce Power

There remains the question whether such restriction on the production of goods for commerce is a permissible exercise of the commerce power. The power of Congress over interstate commerce is not confined to the regulation of commerce among the states. It extends to those activities intrastate which so affect interstate commerce or the exercise of the power of Congress over it as to make regulation of them appropriate means to the attainment of a legitimate end, the exercise of the granted power of Congress to regulate interstate commerce.

While this Court has many times found state regulation of interstate commerce, when uniformity of its regulation is of national concern, to be incompatible with the Commerce Clause even though Congress has not legislated on the subject, the Court has never implied such restraint on state control over matters intrastate not deemed to be regulations of interstate commerce or its instrumentalities even though they affect the commerce. In the absence of Congressional legislation on the subject, state laws which are not regulations of the commerce itself or its instrumentalities are not forbidden, even though they affect interstate commerce.

But it does not follow that Congress may not, by appropriate legislation, regulate intrastate activities where they have a substantial effect on interstate commerce. A recent example is the National Labor Relations Act for the regulation of employer and employee relations in industries in which strikes, induced by unfair labor practices named in the Act, tend to disturb or obstruct interstate commerce. But, long before the adoption of the National Labor Relations Act, this Court had many times held that the power of Congress to regulate interstate commerce extends to the regulation through legislative action of activities intrastate which have a substantial effect on the commerce or the exercise of the Congressional power over it. . . .

The Tenth Amendment Is a Truism

Our conclusion is unaffected by the Tenth Amendment, which provides:

> The powers not delegated to the United States by the Constitution, nor prohibited by it to the States, are reserved to the States respectively, or to the people.

The amendment states but a truism that all is retained which has not been surrendered. There is nothing in the history of its adoption to suggest that it was more than declaratory of the relationship between the national and state governments as it had been established by the Constitution before the amendment, or that its purpose was other than to allay fears that the new national government might seek to exercise powers not granted, and that the states might not be able to exercise fully their reserved powers.

From the beginning and for many years, the amendment has been construed as not depriving the national government of authority to resort to all means for the exercise of a granted power which are appropriate and plainly adapted to the permitted end. Whatever doubts may have arisen of the soundness of that conclusion, they have been put at rest by the decisions under the Sherman Act and the National Labor Relations Act. . . .

Decision Reversed

Validity of the requirement of records of wages and hours. §
15(a)(5) and § 11(c). These requirements are incidental to those for the prescribed wages and hours, and hence validity of the former turns on validity of the latter. Since, as we have held, Congress may require production for interstate commerce to conform to those conditions, it may require the employer, as a means of enforcing the valid law, to keep a record showing whether he has, in fact, complied with it. The requirement for records even of the intrastate transaction is an

appropriate means to the legitimate end.

Validity of the wage and hour provisions under the Fifth Amendment. Both provisions are minimum wage requirements compelling the payment of a minimum standard wage with a prescribed increased wage for overtime of "not less than one and one-half times the regular rate" at which the worker is employed. Since our decision in *West Coast Hotel Co. v. Parrish* [1937], it is no longer open to question that the fixing of a minimum wage is within the legislative power, and that the bare fact of its exercise is not a denial of due process under the Fifth more than under the Fourteenth Amendment. Nor is it any longer open to question that it is within the legislative power to fix maximum hours. Similarly, the statute is not objectionable because applied alike to both men and women.

The Act is sufficiently definite to meet constitutional demands. One who employs persons, without conforming to the prescribed wage and hour conditions, to work on goods which he ships or expects to ship across state lines is warned that he may be subject to the criminal penalties of the Act. No more is required.

We have considered, but find it unnecessary to discuss other contentions.

Reversed.

The Bill of Rights

CHAPTER 3

Major Conflicts Over States' Rights

The Nullification Crisis of 1832–1833

Bernard A. Weisberger

The controversy over states' rights during the 1820s and early 1830s was a noteworthy precursor to the deeper sectional divisions—culminating in civil war—that the nation would face in subsequent decades. States' rights supporters became more vocal and took increasingly concrete actions by enacting the doctrine of nullification, which held that a state could nullify a federal law if it viewed the law as unconstitutional.

In 1828 the so-called "Tariff of Abominations," a tax that protected flourishing New England industry, drew protest from the South. The South was economically depressed and attributed its problems to high-duty tariffs. In response to the mounting southern frustration, South Carolina senator and then–vice president John C. Calhoun secretly authored the South Carolina Exposition and Protest. *Calhoun's work decried the protective tariff as unconstitutional and advanced the theory of nullification.*

The following excerpt from an article by Bernard A. Weisberger describes the atmosphere in which Calhoun's work was written and received. Weisberger suggests that Calhoun's Exposition *is a commentary not only on the tariff issue but also on the balance of power between the state and federal government. Calhoun proposed the remedy of nullification via the interposition of a state veto. In other words, the state would mediate between its citizens and the federal government rather than compel its citizens to comply with what the people of the state considered an unconstitutional law.*

In 1832 Congress made the protective tariff permanent policy; South Carolina enacted the Exposition *principles and brought*

Bernard A. Weisberger,"The Nullifiers," *American Heritage*, vol. 46, October 1995. Copyright © 1995 by *American Heritage*, a Division of Forbes, Inc. Reproduced by permission.

the issue to the people. The state legislature, with the support of the people, declared an Ordinance of Nullification, which rendered the tariffs of 1828 and 1832 unconstitutional and not binding for South Carolina. President Andrew Jackson responded with the Force Act, which denounced nullification as treason and justified the use of military action to enforce the law. In the end, tempers receded as Congress modified the tariff and South Carolina rescinded the ordinance.

Historian Bernard A. Weisberger is the author of more than a dozen books and a contributing editor to the journal American Heritage. *He taught at Wayne State University, the University of Chicago, and the University of Rochester before devoting himself to writing full time.*

One early case of acute States' Rights fever was the so-called nullification crisis of 1832–33. The story—a very dramatic one—is worth retelling for the light it sheds on the complexities of the federal system, as well as for its tangy mixture of principle, greed, ambition, and avarice.

The Constitution Stretched

In its 1827 and 1828 sessions, Congress was debating upward revision of the tariff in force since the end of the War of 1812. The tariff had raised money for important national projects, such as a national road to the West, and it modestly protected the infant U.S. textile industry. In 1816 few South Carolinians had objected—certainly not John C. Calhoun, the vigorous national growth advocate, who became Vice President to John Quincy Adams in 1825. But the 1820s were not kind to South Carolina. Its plantation economy suffered from a depression, while prospering manufacturers began to ask for still more protection. In the election year of 1828 they got the attention of campaign managers of the candidate Andrew Jackson, and in the end they got their high tariff. Jackson won the White House, and Calhoun was again elected Vice President, but his position in the administration was now made ambiguous by his home state's discontent.

Some Carolinians had begun to argue that Congress had stuck planters with a so-called Tariff of Abominations that raised their costs for manufactured goods and lowered foreign demand for their rice and cotton. Worse, the Constitution had been stretched out of shape for the purpose.

Implied Powers?

Nowhere was Congress specifically authorized to levy a tariff. That was simply "implied" in the powers to raise revenue and regulate commerce through laws that were, in the elastic phrase, "necessary and proper" to those ends. As the strict construction critics saw it, this "protective" tariff was an outrageous forced transfer of wealth from one section to another.

Behind the revulsion against the tariff was another anxiety that troubled even Carolinians whose fortunes weren't suffering in 1827. It was slavery. William Smith warned his fellow citizens that the flexible "general welfare" clause in the Constitution's preamble, having already been used to tax them for the benefit of "manufacturers . . . wallowing in wealth" would next allow the "Northern States" to "rend your government asunder, or make slaves your masters."

Constitutional Remedy

Was there constitutional remedy? The tariff rebels thought so. The states—South Carolina included—had created the national government in 1787 and given their consent for it to act as their agent. What was given could also be taken away in whole or in part. Why not simply refuse to honor the presumptuous act of an overreaching agent without firing him—in short, simply "nullify" an unconstitutional exercise of power within South Carolina's boundaries?

Not all Carolinians were convinced. A party of moderates argued that the Supreme Court was the proper place for deciding constitutional issues and that allowing each state in the Union to interpret the document for itself was a recipe for the kind of anarchy that had wrecked the Articles of Confederation. The nullifiers called on Calhoun, South Carolina's most visible and articulate statesman, to speak for them. He agreed with them, but because he still had presidential ambitions, he made his case anonymously, in a document called the South Carolina Exposition and Protest.

Calhoun's Theory

In it Calhoun deftly refined, recast, and actually limited the argument, using the contract theory underlying American constitutionalism. For their mutual safety and advantage, the sovereign people of each state "contracted" away some of their liberty to a central government—the agent that they created. To rebuke an act of that government that overstepped the limits of the contract, they would have to reassemble (through representatives) in a special convention just like the one that had ratified the Constitution—a body superior to any ordinary legislature—and invoke their sovereign right to the last word.

This kind of nullification, the Exposition argued, was unlikely to happen often. It would actually prevent secession, though that was a legitimate last resort. It even left the door open for South Carolina to go along if three-quarters of the states should amend the Constitution. It was, Calhoun insisted to his dying day, a means of preserving the Union as it should be, with all the member states treated fairly.

Reasonable as it sounded, South Carolina voters rejected the nullifiers in 1832 and elected a moderate majority to the state's legislature, which printed the Exposition and Protest but did not call a nullification convention. The moderates' hope was that Calhoun would use his influence in the administration to get the tariff lowered without a clash.

The Union Most Dear

Instead things went terribly wrong. Calhoun and Jackson split on a variety of issues, of which Old Hickory's [Andrew Jackson's nickname] flinty nationalism was only one. Their hardening enmity set up one of those great tableaux that adorned traditional history books: a Democratic-party dinner early in 1830 at which the President, called on for a toast, gazed straight at Calhoun and proposed: "Our Federal Union. It must and shall be preserved." To which the Vice President retorted with unflinching lifted gaze: "The Union—next to our liberties most dear."

By 1832 an isolated Calhoun watched helplessly as Jackson won re-election with a new Vice President, New York's politically astute Martin Van Buren. Continued hard times and increased anxiety over slavery turned the South Carolina tide and swept the nullifiers to victory in state elections. Calhoun was now openly among them, having acknowledged his authorship of the Exposition and Protest and lamenting that pro-tariff nationalists were sacrificing the Union to a passion for riches. "I never suspected that a people could so sadly degenerate," he declared.

Nullifiers in Action

The crisis broke in November 1832, when the special nullification convention was convoked and decreed that after the next February it should "not be lawful . . . to enforce payment to duties . . . within the limits of this state." Any attempt by Congress to use military measures would result in secession. The nullifiers were aflame, but so was Andrew Jackson. In a January message to Congress he proclaimed that nullification was expressly contradicted by the letter and spirit of the Constitution, that "disunion by armed force" was "treason." He called for legislation, known as the Force Bill, to let him use the Army and Navy, if necessary, to deal with the crisis. South Carolina's legislature responded by giving Gov. Robert Hayne the authority to raise state troops, and some twenty-five thousand volunteers were soon drilling the winter away.

But behind the fist shaking on both sides there was some prudence. Early in February 1833 Sen. Henry Clay introduced a plan to slice protective duties in half over a ten-year span, reducing them finally to a level that could be considered "for revenue only." Clay's bill was promptly supported by none other than Sen. John C. Calhoun, who had left the Vice Presidency and had been elected to the Senate by the South Carolina legislature. The revised tariff passed both houses by March 1. The Force Bill—now more symbolic than likely to take effect—passed by big majorities within a week. Calhoun then rushed home to help talk moderation to the reconvened special convention, where extreme nullifiers still threatened secession over the mere threat of national coercion. A compromise finally prevailed. The convention rescinded the offending original ordinance—and then proceeded to "nullify" the Force Bill.

Preserving the Union

So principle was verbally upheld even as the armies marched back downhill. Jackson preserved the Union, and Calhoun could write to a friend that he had "no doubts the [tariff] system has got its death wound" and nullification had dealt "the fatal blow." That's the kind of resolution that I confess I like to see. But it was of course only a short term outcome. In 1860–61 moderation lost and civil war came (followed by high tariffs).

Calhoun had gone to his grave in 1850, staunchly calling for the preservation of the Union by granting the South a veto over federal encroachments on its rights. In my graduate school days he was much admired as a farseeing defender of the claims of a permanent minority within the nation. But even then I simply couldn't divorce his abstractions from their real-life pro-slavery context. So much depends on one's initial prejudices.

Secession Challenges the Tenth Amendment

Daniel Farber

From the 1830s through the 1850s, the debate over states' rights intensified due to the issue of slavery. Territory gained through westward expansion also raised political questions as to whether or not slavery would be permitted in new states as they entered the Union. The North opposed slavery and wanted to prevent its expansion into the western territories, whereas the South believed slavery to be essential to its economic livelihood and considered the cessation of the system a tremendous threat. Hints of sectionalism in previous decades became outright hostility, leading to secession and the Civil War in the 1860s.

In the following excerpt, constitutional scholar Daniel Farber examines the issue that was the most serious constitutional crisis in U.S. history: secession. The North's desire to abolish slavery coupled with the South's fervent demand that the institution remain intact led to the emergence of secessionist political theory. Linked to nullification theory, which advocated the right of states to nullify a federal law, secessionist theory went a step further by endorsing withdrawal and separation from the Union. Those in favor of secession as a political solution to discontent maintained that it was within the rights of the states as an act of self-preservation, and was therefore constitutional. Opponents to secessionist theory claimed that secession was neither a matter of states' rights nor a constitutional act. In their view, secession violated the federal compact of the Union. The debate over secession, then, was ultimately a debate over states' rights. Farber explores the arguments behind each position and describes how the South came to embrace secessionist theory.

Daniel Farber, *Lincoln's Constitution*. Chicago: University of Chicago Press, 2003. Copyright © 2003 by the University of Chicago. All rights reserved. Reproduced by permission.

Daniel Farber is professor of law at the University of California–Berkeley, and at the University of Minnesota. His research focuses on constitutional law, and he is the author of numerous publications, including several books.

Secession obviously brought the debate over states' rights to a feverish level. In many respects, these arguments were replays of the debates over interposition and nullification.[1]

Nullification Versus Secession

But in some respects, secession is actually a tougher legal issue than nullification. Nullification requires state judges to follow the mandates of their state legislatures on constitutional issues, notwithstanding their own contrary views or those of the Supreme Court, thereby blocking the normal process of judicial review. This directly contradicts the supremacy clause's mandate that state judges follow the Constitution regardless of state law. Nullification is also at odds with the federal courts' authority under Article III to decide cases arising under federal law. Secessionist theory, however, is not inconsistent with a qualified form of federal supremacy. Under this view, a state must fully comply with federal law so long as it remains in the Union, just as a citizen must comply with federal law or emigrate elsewhere. Thus, secessionism can give federal supremacy its full scope with respect to whatever states happen to be part of the Union at any given time. Compared with nullification, secession requires less distortion of the constitutional structure—it merely adds an exit option. And unlike national supremacy, secession did not receive much attention from the Framers, so both the constitutional text and the historical record speak less clearly and directly to the issue.

Advocates made two very different kinds of arguments for secession. First, they claimed it was a valid state prerogative

1. Interposition is a means by which a state uses a veto to prevent its people from having to enact or abide by a federal law. Nullification is a state's right to nullify or render void a federal law.

under the Constitution itself. Such an argument could be based on the compact theory that [John C.] Calhoun and others had long espoused. It could also be based on a simple reversal of the act of ratification by which states became bound by the Constitution. Second, advocates defended secession as an extraconstitutional act. Like the Declaration of Independence, secession could be viewed as a justified act of revolution or as an exercise of the inherent right of self-determination. . . .

Slavery and Self-Government

A decade before the Civil War, the Compromise of 1850[2] seemed to have brought peace to the sectional dispute. But when [Illinois representative Stephen A.] Douglas introduced his bill to organize the Kansas and Nebraska territories, he gave way to Southern pressure for more favorable treatment of the slavery question. Setting aside the Missouri Compromise,[3] which would have barred slavery from these areas, he left the status of slavery in the new territories open. Douglas's goal was not to bring slavery into these Western territories. Rather, he considered the issue of little practical importance, doubting that slavery had any chance to take root there anyway. In repealing the Missouri Compromise, Douglas himself was merely accommodating strong Southern opposition to any territorial bill formally excluding slavery from the territories. He was much more intent on clearing the way for construction of a transcontinental railroad. But this turned out to be a terrible strategic error. It aroused a crescendo of protest in the North, and more than anything else, led to the creation of the Republican party.

2. The Compromise of 1850 was a bill that organized territories into slave or free states and that firmed up fugitive slave laws.

3. The Missouri Compromise (1820) admitted states north of Missouri's southern border as free states.

The Kansas-Nebraska Bill[4] energized men like [Abraham] Lincoln and pushed them toward the formation of a new "anti-Nebraska" party. Although the bill purported to be indifferent to the spread of slavery, Lincoln said that in reality it shifted the balance toward slavery. He angrily rejected this favorable treatment of slavery "because of the monstrous injustice of slavery itself" and because it "deprives our republican example of its just influence in the world." He acknowledged that eliminating the institution where it already existed would pose great difficulties for the South, with which he sympathized. But the difficulty of abolition furnished no more of an excuse for extending slavery than it would for reviving the African slave trade. In the Framers' time, slavery was a necessary evil, which they prohibited in the Northwest territory where it had not yet taken hold. "But NOW," slavery was "to be transformed into a 'sacred right.'" "Near[ly] eighty years ago," Lincoln observed, "we began by declaring that all men are created equal; but now from that beginning we have run down to the other declaration, that for SOME MEN to enslave OTHERS is a 'sacred right of self-government.'" "These principles," he added, "can not stand together." He called on his audience to return slavery "to the position our fathers gave it," as a sad necessity where it already existed, "and there let it rest in peace."

Southern Influence on National Government

The Republican platform included provisions on the federal budget, naturalization, a Pacific railroad, and other issues. Undoubtedly, these issues were more important to some supporters than slavery. But it was the slavery issue that defined the party. Republicans opposed slavery for a variety of reasons, moral, economic, and political. Lincoln spoke for many Republicans in calling slavery a betrayal of the American creed that "all men are created equal." Economically, slavery was

4. The Kansas-Nebraska Bill allowed Kansas and Nebraska to leave their free or slave state status up to the people via popular sovereignty.

considered to be a barrier to economic development and a handicap to white farmers and workers. Antislavery writers compared Northern economic dynamism to the sleepy Southern agrarian economy. They also denounced the unfairness of requiring whites to compete against slave labor. Finally, Republicans feared that the country was coming under the grip of the Slavocracy, a powerful elite whose members were morally corrupted by their absolute power over slaves. Through its control of the Democratic party, its representation in the Senate, and its overrepresentation in the House under the three-fifths rule, the slave power had supposedly seized control of the country. In the Lincoln-Douglas debates[5] Lincoln portrayed his opponent as a supporter of a Southern conspiracy to extend slavery nationwide. Although no organized conspiracy actually existed, Southern slaveholders did have a formidable influence on the national government. . . .

Growing Sectionalism

The South resented restrictions on slavery as a slight to its honor. In [Thomas] Jefferson's time, Southerners had considered slavery a necessary evil, imposed on them by history. Jefferson and others predicted its ultimate extinction. But by the 1850s, leading Southerners proclaimed slavery to be a positive good. For whites, they said, it provided the basis of a distinctive civilization, for blacks, paternalistic and much needed guidance from a superior race. Excluding slavery from the territories sent the message that slavery, the whole basis of the Southern way of life, was immoral and degrading. This was an affront to Southern pride.

The South became more demanding of Northern support for slavery. At the time of the Missouri Compromise, the South was willing to accept the exclusion of slavery from some territories. By the time of the Kansas-Nebraska Bill, the

5. The Lincoln-Douglas debates took place during the 1858 senatorial campaign. Abraham Lincoln, the Republican candidate, and Stephen Douglas, the Democrat incumbent, debated over the slavery issue and sectionalism.

South was demanding popular sovereignty, which would leave all the territories potentially open to slaveholders. Later, even this was not enough. Fearing that hostile territorial legislatures would either outlaw slavery or fail to give it legal protection, Southerners wanted affirmative congressional legislation protecting slavery in the territories.

The quarrel over slavery in the territories came to a head, fittingly enough, in Charleston. Although Charleston's connection with secession is best known because the Civil War broke out there, another event in that city a year or so earlier was equally critical: the breakup of the Democratic party's presidential convention. The delegates arrived in late April [1860], almost exactly a year before Sumter.[6]
Douglas entered the convention with a clear majority but less than the two-thirds required under party rules. The critical battle involved the platform. Douglas was the leading advocate of popular sovereignty, under which the people of each territory would decide the slavery issue. But this position was unacceptable to many Democrats in the South, who demanded a congressional slave code. Douglas had sworn to refuse the nomination if the platform endorsed such a slave code, while Alabama and others threatened to withdraw from the convention unless the slave code was endorsed. After the slave code provision failed, Alabama, Arkansas, Florida, Georgia, Louisiana, Mississippi, South Carolina, and Texas walked out. In June, the convention met again in Baltimore, with even worse results. California, North Carolina, Oregon, Tennessee, and Virginia also bolted, along with most of the Arkansas, Kentucky, and Missouri delegations. The bolters held their own convention, which adopted a platform endorsing the slave code and nominated [John] Breckinridge for the presidency. The walkout shattered the party, destroying the last remaining

6. On April 12, 1861, the Southern states that seceded from the Union and formed the Confederacy fired on Fort Sumter in South Carolina. This act against a U.S. military fort ignited the Civil War.

nonsectional political coalition, and paved the way for Lincoln's election.

Secessionist Ideas

A small but important group of Southerners welcomed, and had even planned for, this development. Southern fire-eaters had long favored secession and had sought unsuccessfully to goad their compatriots into action. They foresaw that insistence on a slave code would fracture the Democratic party and lead to a Republican victory, which would be intolerable to many Southerners. With luck, the result would be Southern independence.

As the election approached, speeches and articles throughout the South warned of secession. When Lincoln's election became certain, the Deep South, particularly South Carolina, went into a frenzy. The South Carolina legislature, which had been in session to choose presidential electors, authorized the governor to spend one hundred thousand dollars for arms. It set December 6 as the date to elect representatives for a special convention on December 17. Mass rallies in Georgia, Alabama, and Mississippi called for immediate secession. By the end of November, Mississippi, Alabama, and Georgia had also made arrangements for state secession conventions.

Secessionists warned that the Republicans would soon control both houses of Congress, as well as the presidency. They would ban slavery wherever the federal government had jurisdiction and would continue admitting free states until they had enough of a majority to amend the Constitution and abolish slavery nationally. Even limiting slavery geographically would be a disaster. As the black population continued to grow, a race war would break out, and either blacks would be wiped out or whites would be forced to leave. Secessionists also recalled other grievances such as the tariff.[7]

---

7. The tariff issue, represented by several tax laws in the late 1820s and early 1830s, was supported by the Northern states and resented by the Southern states.

In contrast to the South's current woes, secession promised a new era of prosperity and expansion. Secessionists looked forward to the day when Southern civilization would extend "across [the American] continent to the Pacific, and down through Mexico to the other side of the great gulf, and over the isles of the sea." [Allan Nevins]

Buchanan's Response

Whatever may be said of these dreams of glory, modern historians do not view the South's fear of a Republican presidency as wholly ungrounded. Because of the "monolithic, closed system of social and intellectual arrangements upon which the South relied for the perpetuation of slavery" [David Potter], the Republicans could disrupt the South without new legislation, simply by using federal patronage and control of the mails to foster the growth of white opposition. Moreover, as one historian [Richard Sewall] explains, Southerners felt that the North's election of Lincoln "grossly insulted the South and proclaimed its determination to make vassals—slaves—of Southern whites."

The [James] Buchanan administration responded hesitantly to the secession movement. On November 20, Attorney General [Jeremiah Sullivan] Black issued a formal opinion about secession. Black viewed the president as having little power to block secession. He did advise Buchanan that he could defend and even retake federal property. (As an example of the government's power to retake property, he pointed to Harpers Ferry, where U.S. troops under the control of Robert E. Lee had retaken the federal armory after it was seized by John Brown.) But that, he said, was the limit of the government's coercive power. The president could call out the militia to assist federal judges and revenue collectors in enforcing the law, but if these individuals all resigned (as seemed likely in the event of secession), there would be no legal enforcement actions for the militia to assist. If troops are to be "sent to aid the courts and marshals, there must be courts and marshals to be aided." Thus, the president could do little about secession except to denounce it. On the one hand, he could not acknowledge any state as independent. On the other hand, neither he nor Congress could "make war" against any of the states, so as to coerce it into rejoining the Union.

The attorney general's opinion became the basis for President Buchanan's major statement about secession on December 3. Buchanan blamed the North for the crisis. The South had been patient during repeated Northern assaults on its rights, but Southerners could tolerate no more abuse when their families' safety was threatened. "The immediate peril" to the South, Buchanan said, arose "from the fact that the incessant and violent agitation of the slavery question throughout the North for the last quarter of a century has at length produced its malign influence on the slaves, and inspired them with vague notions of freedom." As a result, "Many a matron throughout the South retires at night in dread of what may befall herself and her children before the morning." Yet secession was the wrong remedy. Although the South's grievances were legitimate and should be met with constitutional amendments providing greater security for slavery, secession was unlawful. The president was entitled to maintain possession of U.S. property, which had been purchased at a fair price. But this was strictly a defensive power. The Constitution did not empower the federal government "to make war against a State." Buchanan's goal was to conciliate the South, simultaneously arguing against secession and maintaining the government's rights over its own property. Buchanan's speech has been called [by Don Fehrenbacher] a "confession of national impotence" and "the last major act of the federal government truly serving the slaveholder interest."

The Union Dissolved

By Christmas, South Carolina had seceded. Its "Declaration of the Causes of Secession" argued that the Northern states had breached their constitutional obligations. The North had "denounced as sinful the institution of Slavery," had "permitted the open establishment among them" of antislavery societies, and had "encouraged and assisted thousands of our slaves to leave their homes; and those who remain have been incited by emissaries, books, and pictures, to servile insurrection." With a sectional party about to seize control of the federal government, the South Carolina declaration proclaimed, the South was in grave peril. For that party's nefarious program was to exclude the South "from the common territory," make over the Supreme Court, and ultimately eliminate slavery. "We, therefore, the people of South Carolina, by our delegates in Convention assembled," have declared the Union dissolved.

Within a few weeks, the gulf states had followed South Carolina out of the Union. By February the Confederate States of America had adopted a provisional constitution and had elected Jefferson Davis as president. But the slaveholding states of the upper South balked, though they did vow to resist federal coercion of the seceding states. The newly born Confederacy was highly vulnerable without the support of Virginia and the rest of the upper South. Secessionist stalwarts urged an attack on Fort Sumter to rally the South in support of secession.

On April 12, 1861, Confederate forces opened fire on Fort Sumter. The rest, as they say, is history.

Davis's Secession Theory

Jefferson Davis defended the constitutionality of secession in a speech shortly after Sumter. Like Calhoun, he relied on the compact theory of the Constitution. During the Revolution, he said, the British threat led the states to a "close alliance" and to the formation of a confederation under which each state expressly reserved its rights of sovereignty. The war was won under this "contract of alliance." In 1787, the "several States" appointed delegates to the Constitutional Convention, and the Constitution was then ratified by the "several States." The fact that the Constitution became effective only between those states that ratified showed its "true character—that of a *compact between* independent States." But "some alarm was felt in the States" because the sovereignty guarantees of the Articles had been omitted. The states did not rest until amendments placed "beyond any pretense of doubt the reservation by the States of all their sovereign rights and powers not expressly delegated to the United States by the Constitution."

Alas, Davis said, "all these carefully worded clauses proved unavailing" against the rise of a Northern heresy, which held that the Constitution did not create a compact of states but rather "in effect a national government." Indeed, "so utterly have the principles of the Constitution been corrupted in the Northern mind" that Lincoln had asserted "as an axiom" that the Constitution was based on majority rule. In the meantime, the North was not honoring its side of the constitutional bargain. Although the Constitution had contained several clauses endorsing slavery, the North had turned against the South. In a "display of a spirit of ultra fanaticism," Northern representatives attacked the vital interests of the South. Finally, a new party had gained power "with the avowed object of using its power for the total exclusion of the slave States from all participation in the benefits of the public domain acquired by all the States in common, whether by conquest or purchase; of surrounding them entirely by States in which slavery should be prohibited; of thus rendering the property in slaves so insecure as to be comparatively worthless, and thereby annihilating in effect property worth thousands of millions of dollars."

The Primacy of States' Rights

Southern legislatures, Davis continued, had then invited the sovereign people to select delegates for state conventions to determine the proper response. In this, Davis insisted, they were following a long-established tradition. "From a period as early as 1798," the majority party nationally (the Democrats) had adopted the "creed that each State was, in the last resort, the sole judge as well of its wrongs as of the mode and measure of redress." Indeed, Davis said, "it is obvious that under the law of nations this principle is an axiom as applied to the relations of independent sovereign States, such as those which had united themselves under the constitutional compact." (Here, he relied on the Kentucky and Virginia Resolutions[8] and on [James] Madison's response to criticism from other state legislatures.) Exercising this power, the Southern state conventions had decided on secession.

After the Civil War, Jefferson Davis's vice president, Alexander H. Stephens, presented a far more elaborate version of Davis's arguments, which became the postwar Southern orthodoxy. Although much more detailed and heavily documented, the heart of Stephens's argument was the same. He maintained that "absolute right of local Self Government, or State Sovereignty, was the primal and leading idea throughout" the formation of the Union. The Union was only an "artificial or conventional Nation" created for certain limited purposes such as foreign relations. "Can any proposition within the domain of reason be clearer," he asked, "than that the Sovereignty of the States, that great Paramount authority which can rightfully make and unmake Constitutions, resides still with the States?" As to secession, it is "the inherent right of Nations" to "disregard the obligations of Compacts of all sorts, by declaring themselves no longer bound in any way by them." Disowning a compact is proper whenever "there has been a breach of the Compact by the other party or parties." The refusal of Northern states to comply with their obligation to return fugitive slaves was itself a sufficient breach of the compact to justify secession. By way of Stephens's later exege-

8. The Kentucky and Virginia Resolutions of 1798 and 1799 advocated a states' rights position and insisted that federal power should not reach past what the Constitution explicitly states.

sis, the same arguments made by Davis in 1861 became an article of faith among many Southerners long afterward.

Perpetual Union

The Northern view was much different. Lincoln had presented his view of secession in his own inaugural address, partly in response to an earlier speech by Davis. He began with the proposition that "[p]erpetuity is implied, if not expressed, in the fundamental law of all national governments." Even if the "United States be not a government proper, but an association of States in the nature of contract merely," a contract cannot be rescinded without the consent of all of the parties.

"Descending from these general principles," Lincoln contended that the history of the Union confirmed its perpetuity. "The Union is much older than the Constitution." "It was formed in fact" in 1774 by the Articles of Association, "matured and continued" by the Declaration of Independence, and further matured by the Articles of Confederation, in which the states "expressly plighted and engaged that it should be perpetual." Finally, the Constitution was ordained "to form a more perfect union." But, Lincoln continued, if the Union could be destroyed by one or more states, "the Union is *less* perfect than before the Constitution, having lost the vital element of perpetuity."

True, Lincoln admitted, if a majority deprived a minority "of any clearly written constitutional right, it might, in a moral point of view, justify revolution—certainly would, if such right were a vital one." But no such claim could be made by the South. At most, there was a reasonable difference in opinion about constitutional issues. If minorities seceded over every dispute about the meaning of the Constitution, democracy would be impossible. "Plainly," he said, "the central idea of secession, is the essence of anarchy." The "only true sovereign of a free people" is a majority "held in restraint by constitutional checks, and limitations, and always changing easily, with deliberate changes of popular opinions and sentiments."

History is written by the victors, and the idea of secession has been dead since Appomattox. But Jefferson Davis's view of the Constitution was not a frivolous one. Compact theory had been an important current in American constitutional thought since at least 1798. We have already seen that the evolution of sovereignty in the United States was complex and ambiguous; Davis's view of that evolution was not completely lacking in historical support.

Invoking State Sovereignty to Resist Federal Civil Rights Laws

Yasuhiro Katagiri

For more than a hundred years after the Civil War, the United States faced race relations problems. Although blacks gained freedom, they often did not enjoy peaceful coexistence with their white neighbors. The southern states in particular were hostile to blacks and over time enacted numerous discriminatory laws and policies. Additionally, the racial tensions frequently resulted in violence directed at blacks.

Thus, a segregationist culture became entrenched in American society. By the mid-twentieth century, a civil rights movement emerged, urging equality among the races and the end of segregation. The federal government eventually heeded the message of the civil rights activists, promoted the necessary changes, and pressured states to end segregation.

A key turning point in the civil rights movement was the Supreme Court's decision in Brown v. Board of Education *(1954), which outlawed segregation in public schools. The federal mandate was not well-received by some states, as evidenced by the "Southern Manifesto," a document drafted by politicians in eleven southern states in protest to the* Brown *ruling. Riots in both Central High School in Little Rock, Arkansas (1957), and the University of Mississippi (1962) resulted in the use of federal troops to enforce desegregation.*

In the following excerpt, historian Yasuhiro Katagiri discusses the response of one state—Mississippi—to the federal government's demands during the heyday of the civil rights

Yasuhiro Katagiri, "With the Aura of Sophistication and Respectability: The Mississippi State Sovereignty Commission and Its Use of Constitutional Discourse Against the Civil Rights Movement," paper presented at the Annual Meeting of the Organization of American Historians, March 27, 2004, Boston, MA.Copyright © 2004 by Yasuhiro Katagiri. Reproduced by permission.

movement in the 1950s and 1960s. Mississippi rejected the Court's ruling in Brown *as a violation of its right to educate its citizens as it saw fit. Katagiri writes that in a defiant and bold act of states' rights advocacy, the state created a "state sovereignty commission" in an effort to preserve Mississippi's segregationist norms despite federal rulings. He offers a brief history of the commission and of the state's role of resistance to the civil rights movement.*

Mississippi, along with all the other states, was ultimately compelled to comply with federal legislation on civil rights. Federal authority was supreme in this matter regardless of the cultures of individual states.

Yasuhiro Katagiri is an associate professor of American history and government at Tokai University in Kanagawa, Japan. He is the author of a book on the Mississippi State Sovereignty Commission.

On Monday, May 17, 1954, the United States Supreme Court unanimously outlawed legally imposed racial segregation in public schools in *Brown v. Board of Education.* For Judge Robert L. Carter, who had led the litigation as an attorney for the National Association for the Advancement of Colored People (NAACP), the day would always be treasured as a very special one when the Supreme Court finally rendered "the highest pinnacle of American judicial expression" and espoused the nation's "loftiest values." But for the vast majority of white southerners, the same day would soon be remembered in disgust as "Black Monday"—a phrase which was originally coined by United States Representative John Bell Williams from Mississippi, a future governor of the state, and "was to stick as a Southern epithet" [as stated by journalist Hodding Carter].

Resurrecting States' Rights Theory

Resenting and even despising this voice of American conscience raised by the nation's highest tribunal, some white southerners advocated that racial segregation, crucial to perpetuating their cherished "southern way of life," was God-ordained and predestined, and some, even though they were relatively small in number, resorted to economic intimidation and abominable violence to defend the region's racial status quo. Still others blindly and blatantly resorted to the assertion that black southerners' quest for social justice and simple human dignity was nothing more than a foreign enterprise both directed and dominated by despicable "Communist" agitators and subversives. More important, however, southern white leadership resurrected and reintroduced a seemingly more sophisticated theory of states' rights constitutionalism to negate the Supreme Court decree and to crack down on the ever-intensifying civil rights movement in the South.

By whatever means they chose to defend their segregated societies, the majority of white southerners were fearful of the unforeseeable consequences that the *Brown* decision, the Supreme Court, and the federal government as a whole would bring about in southern societies. White southerners—politicians and ordinary citizens alike—thus formed and carried out [what U.S. Senator Harry F. Byrd called] the region's "massive resistance" to what they perceived as "federal encroachment" on their way of life.

Resistance to Federal Pressure

Describing some striking characteristics of Mississippi politics in his *Southern Politics in State and Nation*, V.O. Key, Jr., a gifted political scientist, offered a keen observation in 1949 that "the beginning and the end of Mississippi politics is the Negro." In this groundbreaking study, which was published only a year after the 1948 Dixiecrat revolt bringing forth the States' Rights Democratic Party, Key further went on to predict that Mississippi would carry out "massive resistance" to any "external intervention" that was represented by federally exerted pressures on the state's racial norms.

As if to vindicate this prediction, Mississippi eventually became the most emphatic leader of the "massive resistance" movement in the South both officially and privately. In private spheres, the state became the birthplace of the Citizens' Council in the summer of 1954—the most vocal and widespread organization dedicated to the segregationist cause and anti-*Brown* enterprises. Symbolizing and even personifying the defender of the "southern way of life," the Citizens' Council appropriately adopted and used the words "states' rights" and "racial integrity" on its organizational emblem. By early 1955, the political influence exerted by the Citizens' Council, which was ostensibly a "non-political" grassroots organization, began to steal over the government of Mississippi—"the Council's mother state," to borrow the words of historian Neil R. McMillen.

The Interposition Resolution

Meanwhile, an overwhelming mood of defiance to the federal government dominated the 1956 Mississippi legislative session, where it witnessed the introduction of a parade of bills and resolutions devised to preserve and protect the state's racial norms and sovereignty. Among them, Mississippi's officially sanctioned resistance to the *Brown* ruling manifested itself in the adoption of the so-called interposition resolution.

The preparation for the interposition resolution began in late January 1956, when the state legislature appointed a thirteen-member joint legislative committee to draft the resolution. State Senator Earl Evans, the president pro tempore of the upper House, became chair of the joint committee, or the Committee on Interposition. On February 29, 1956, in submitting the committee's report to the legislature, Chairman Evans, standing on the Senate floor, explained that the "only [legal] approach" that Mississippi would be able to depend upon in defense of its state sovereignty and racial integrity was found in "what Jefferson, Madison, and Calhoun and many others termed 'the Right of Interposition,'" which "still remains [effective] though it has not been used in some eighty years."

Following Chairman Evans's elevated proposal, as if to reveal its adamant determination, the entire forty-nine-member Senate introduced and adopted the state's interposition resolution, which provided: "That the State of Mississippi has at no time, through the Fourteenth Amendment to the Constitution of the United States, or in any manner whatsoever, delegated to the Federal Government its right to educate and nurture its youth. . . ." Noting further that "a question of contested power has arisen" between Mississippi and the federal governments, it declared that Mississippi had the right "to interpose for arresting the progress of the evil." Finally, the resolution asserted the state's "firm intention to take all appropriate measures honorably and constitutionally" to "void this illegal encroachment" upon the rights reserved to Mississippi.

Creating the State Sovereignty Commission

The interposition resolution was immediately sent to the House for its consideration, and the lower House also concurred by a vote of 137 to 0. When the bill passed, five House members stood up on the floor and broke into a chorus of "Dixie." Thus, the resolution—the state's official declaration to refuse to recognize the Supreme Court's *Brown* decision—handily passed both Houses. The nation's High Court rendered what Richard Kluger termed "simple justice" in the school desegregation ruling, but for the vast majority of white Mississippians, it was not "simple" but "sordid" justice by the federal tyranny.

With the defiance to the federal government at its height and inspired by the issuance of the interposition resolution, Mississippi lawmakers now turned to creating a tax-supported implementation agency of the resolves expressed in the resolution. Accordingly, on March 29, 1956, the state created the twelve-member Mississippi State Sovereignty Commission as part of the executive branch of the state government.

Despite the fact that the State Sovereignty Commission was soon to be identified as Mississippi's "segregation watchdog agency," neither the word "segregation" nor the word "integration" appeared in the carefully crafted bill that created the state agency. "It shall be the duty of the commission," the bill provided, "to do and perform any and all acts . . . to protect the sovereignty of the State of Mississippi . . . from encroachment thereon by the Federal Government."

Maintaining Segregation

But to be sure, federal "encroachment" was a periphrasis implying "forced racial integration," and "to protect the sovereignty" of Mississippi from that "encroachment" was a sophisticated roundabout expression of the state's resolve "to preserve and protect the racial segregation" in Mississippi. With the aura of sophistication and respectability emanating from the word "sovereignty," the State Sovereignty Commission, for all practical purposes, was expected to do something unrespectable—[as the commission stated] "to maintain segregation" in Mississippi and to wreck "the NAACP and any other organization . . . attempting to advocate integration and trampling" the rights reserved to the state. While the "encroachment" embodied the watchword of the day, white Mississippians, in the eyes of the nation and the rest of the world, became once again an embattled minority.

Since its inception in 1956 until its practical demise in the late 1960s, the Mississippi State Sovereignty Commission had been composed of two major departments—the public relations and investigative departments. In the early 1960s, the State Sovereignty Commission attained its heyday when Governor Ross R. Barnett took the helm of Mississippi and became chair of the state agency. Having been elected to the governorship with the enthusiastic endorsement of the "non-political" Citizens' Council, Barnett took a solemn pledge in his inaugural address in January 1960. "You know and I know," the governor reminded his fellow white citizens, "that we will maintain segregation in Mississippi at all costs."

Public Relations and Propaganda

True to his own inaugural vow, Governor Barnett, who was an ardent and unreconstructed segregationist as well as a staunch anti-Communist, hammered down on rigid racial segregation with his fanatical preoccupation with defending "Mississippi's way of life." In its "progress report" released at the Mississippi State Sovereignty Commission's March 1961 meeting, the state agency disclosed that it had been "engaged in a detailed investigati[ve] program" to compile a host of files on individuals, whose "utterances or actions indicate they should be watched with suspicion on future racial attitudes." By this time, the State Sovereignty Commission had conducted some 230 "investigations" in all of Mississippi's eighty-two counties.

The state agency's public relations activities were in high gear as well under the chairmanship of Governor Barnett. Disseminating a countless number of pamphlets and other forms of direct mail among the newspaper editors, television stations, and state and national lawmakers above the Mason-Dixon line, the State Sovereignty Commission made every effort to convince non-southerners of the sanity of what Mississippi historian James W. Silver precisely termed the state's "closed society."

But the Mississippi State Sovereignty Commission's most publicized propaganda stunt was the creation of its speakers bureau program in the summer of 1960. The bureau's speakers included state officials, legislators, judges, attorneys, newspaper editors, and businesspeople, and they were dispatched to northern and western states to "sell Mississippi." By the time the speakers bureau was virtually discontinued in the early summer of 1963 due largely to the wretched consequences of the 1962 University of Mississippi desegregation crisis,[1] the State Sovereignty Commission had sent some 100 speakers to approximately 120 speaking engagements before northern and western audiences. . . .

State Sovereignty or Closed Society?

The birth, life, and death of the Mississippi State Sovereignty Commission were the end result of an unsavory segregationist enterprise staged by leading Mississippi white officials. But much more importantly, the very tragedy of its existence was that the State Sovereignty Commission used the constitutional cloak of "state sovereignty" to try to vindicate and perpetuate white Mississippi's inhumane treatment of the state's black citizens. By the time it was finally terminated in 1973, Mississippi's "segregation watchdog agency" had ended up spending over $1.5 million of the state taxpayers' money to keep tabs on and deprive the constitutional rights of its own financial benefactors.

Meanwhile, in the same year the Mississippi State Sovereignty Commission faded away, Bobby Braddock, a country singer from Florida, wrote a song called "I Believe the South Is Gonna Rise Again," embodying white southerners' uncertain search for redemption and reconciliation. . . .

In the end, Mississippi's "massive resistance" under the guise of states' rights ideology had become "massive fallacy" by the middle of the 1970s. The Mississippi State Sovereignty Commission—the keeper of the state's "closed society"—had also come and gone. However, as the words in "Dixie" go, "old times there" are still "not forgotten." And for the fruits of defiance and the liquidation of the resistance movement's dark legacies, Mississippi, to this day, still struggles. The state still struggles because it has not yet fulfilled what country singer Braddock envisioned in his song.

---

1. In 1962, James Meredith became the first black student to enroll at the University of Mississippi. Protected by desegregation laws yet opposed by Mississippi's governor, Meredith's enrollment triggered violent campus riots and required enforcement by federal troops.

Modern Perspectives on the State-Federal Relationship

The Federal and State Roles in Same-Sex Marriage Laws

Cass R. Sunstein

Modern interpretations of the Tenth Amendment continue to challenge the nature of the state-federal relationship, and court cases remain essential to these interpretations and challenges. Throughout the course of the twentieth century, court cases relevant to states' rights extended beyond economic and commercial issues. Social issues also came within the purview of the Tenth Amendment's applicability. Because the U.S. Constitution does not single out many of the social issues that exist in the modern world, the states have the power to decide on such matters independently, as long as federal laws are not violated.

One recent issue to enter the political arena is same-sex marriage. A controversial topic, same-sex marriage is subject to state constitutional laws and is not addressed in the U.S. Constitution. The following article by Cass R. Sunstein is a commentary on the Massachusetts case Goodridge v. Department of Public Health, *which ended a state ban on same-sex marriage. In addition to examining the details and precedents of the case, Sunstein considers the ramifications of the ruling, both on other states and on the state-federal relationship. Above all, Sunstein argues, the decision demonstrates that America's federalist system of government is effective because it allows individual states to establish social policies that are appropriate for their distinct cultures.*

Cass R. Sunstein, whose research focuses on constitutional law, is Karl N. Llewellyn Distinguished Service Professor of Jurisprudence at the Law School and department of political science at the University of Chicago. He is the author or editor of more than a dozen books and has published numerous articles.

Cass R. Sunstein, "Federal Appeal—Massachusetts Gets It Right." *The New Republic*, December 22, 2003, p. 21. Copyright © 2003 by The New Republic, Inc. Reproduced by permission.

In its extraordinary decision in *Goodridge v. Department of Public Health* last month [November 2003], the Massachusetts Supreme Judicial Court ruled that a prohibition on same-sex marriage violates the Massachusetts constitution. While the court drew some support from federal precedents, its decision was plainly grounded in previous interpretations of the state constitution and its distinctive guarantees of equality and liberty. The U.S. Constitution was not involved; it was state—not federal—law that formed the basis for this ruling. We should therefore celebrate *Goodridge*, not only because it ends a form of second-class citizenship for gays and lesbians but also because it exemplifies the federal system at its best.

Precedents in Massachusetts Law

The Massachusetts court's most important conclusion in *Goodridge* was that the state had failed to produce a "rational basis" for its refusal to allow same-sex couples to marry. The state had defended its prohibition of gay marriage principally by arguing that it sought to maintain a "favorable setting for procreation." But, given Massachusetts law, that is a ludicrous explanation. For well over a century, Massachusetts has held that a marriage need not be consummated to be valid. It even allows same-sex couples to have insurance coverage for assisted reproductive technology. In the court's words, the "Commonwealth affirmatively facilitates bringing children into a family regardless of whether the intended parent is married or unmarried . . . and whether the parent or her parent is heterosexual, homosexual, or bisexual."

The state also defended its ban by claiming that it sought an "optimal setting for child rearing," which it defined as "a two-parent family with one parent of each sex." But this rationale is equally difficult to square with Massachusetts's laws and precedents, which recognize and attempt to protect many families that do not fit the traditional mold. For example, in 1983 the court ruled that homosexual orientation is not sufficient grounds for denying child custody in a divorce case; a 1999 decision, also involving child custody, emphasized that the child's best interests should take full account of the child's relationship with "de facto same-sex parents." Furthermore, Massachusetts ensures that adoption is available to married couples and same-sex couples alike. As the court concluded in *Goodridge*, the state's lawyers "offered purported justifications for the civil marriage restriction that are starkly at odds with" Massachusetts's distinctive effort to provide a "comprehensive network of vigorous, gender-neutral laws promoting stable families and the best interests of children." And, in any case, "the task of child rearing for same-sex couples is made infinitely harder by their status as outliers to the marriage laws," not least because of the significant economic and social benefits of marriage under state law.

Judicial or Political Controversy?

Despite the decision's logic, it is tempting to criticize *Goodridge* as an illegitimate judicial intervention into a controversy that should be settled politically. And, to be sure, it would be preferable if gay marriage had been ratified by the Massachusetts legislature rather than the state supreme court. Judges, after all, should not lightly take sides in any "culture war," nor should they try to engineer social change by exploiting ambiguous constitutional provisions. (This was a serious problem in *Roe v. Wade*, where the U.S. Supreme Court used the due process clause as the basis for a broad ruling on behalf of the right to choose.) But these strictures against judicial activism lose much of their force if state judges are simply interpreting state law—as they were in this case—and if the ruling does not foreclose continuing debate within the state. And, in *Goodridge*, the Massachusetts court went out of its way not to foreclose further debate, taking the extraordinary step of delaying its decision for 180 days "to permit the Legislature to take such action as it may deem appropriate in light

Massachusetts was the first state in the country to legally sanction same-sex marriage. ©
Rick Friedman/CORBIS

of this opinion." What does this mean? Well, the ruling says
that the state constitution would not permit the state to bar
"an individual from the protections, benefits, and obligations
of civil marriage solely because that person would marry a
person of the same sex." While this is open to interpretation,
the court appears to be saying that the Massachusetts legislature could satisfy its constitutional duty by recognizing civil
unions—so long as they provided the "protections, benefits,
and obligations of civil marriage"—without necessarily calling
them "marriage."

Moreover, should the state wish to reject *Goodridge* in its
entirety, it could amend the Massachusetts constitution fairly
easily. The process is time-consuming but less arduous than
changing many state constitutions. To get on the ballot, it is
enough for an amendment to be approved by merely one-
quarter of state legislators in two successive legislative sessions

and then to be ratified by a bare majority of Massachusetts voters in a statewide election. Such amendments are not unusual in Massachusetts, where the constitution has been changed 55 times since 1919—sometimes in response to actual or anticipated decisions of the state supreme court. Most prominently, the state constitution was amended in 1982 to authorize capital punishment when the state supreme court was expected to invalidate it. Massachusetts Governor Mitt Romney, along with many others, has already indicated his support for an amendment that would outlaw gay marriage. If the court's decision stands, it will be because these efforts to pass an amendment have failed, demonstrating that Massachusetts voters do not fundamentally object to gay marriage.

The Supreme Court Should Step Back

The reasonableness of the Massachusetts court's decision does not, however, mean the U.S. Supreme Court should follow suit now or in the near future. Quite the contrary. At the national level, judges ought to show caution in ruling on gay rights. To date, that is exactly what they have done—in marked contrast, it should be noted, to *Roe v. Wade*, in which the Court attempted to settle public debate over abortion with one bold stroke. Instead, during the last 15 years, the U.S. Supreme Court has entered the fray over gay rights exactly twice. In its 1996 decision in *Romer v. Evans*, the Court struck down a bizarre amendment to the Colorado constitution that banned the state and its cities and localities from outlawing discrimination against homosexuals. The Court's narrow ruling emphasized that this provision had the "peculiar property of imposing a broad and undifferentiated disability on a single named group." In *Lawrence v. Texas*, decided last summer [2003], the Court took another small step, concluding that states could not punish people engaging in consensual sex. Demonstrating its sensitivity to the importance of procedural legitimacy, the Court stressed that anti-sodomy laws utterly lack popular support, as reflected by the fact that they have fallen into a "pattern of nonenforcement" in the few states where they remained on the books.

Meanwhile, the Court has declined to intervene in the gay rights debates over which the nation is most sharply divided. It has not said a word about same-sex marriage, child custody, discrimination by public employers, and "don't ask, don't tell." In fact, the U.S. Supreme Court has been at most a bit player in what appears to be a genuine revolution in the legal status of American gays and lesbians; it is the states that have taken the major strides. (For example, California, Connecticut, Hawaii, Massachusetts, Minnesota, Nevada, New Hampshire, New Jersey, Rhode Island, and Vermont, among others, now forbid employers to discriminate on the basis of sexual orientation.) And this is how it should be. An attempt by the U.S. Supreme Court to settle the same-sex marriage debate at this time would be disastrous, undoubtedly causing a heated public backlash and endangering the cause of gay rights itself. The genius of the federal system lies in the fact that, while requiring nationwide respect for certain rights, it allows the law to adapt to the states' diverse cultures, providing extensive room for experimentation and learning. This process should be allowed to run its course before the U.S. Supreme Court weighs in.

Must Marriages Be Recognized in Other States?

Of course, such state-level experimentation will lead to different laws, raising one obvious question: Must other states recognize same-sex marriages conducted in Massachusetts? If so, Massachusetts would be effectively setting marriage policy for the nation. And, indeed, the U.S. Constitution's Full Faith and Credit Clause does require each state to respect the "public Acts, Records, and judicial Proceedings of every other state."

But, well before *Goodridge* was decided, Massachusetts law provided that out-of-state visitors could not marry in Massachusetts when the union would be invalid in their state of residence. In any case, Congress foresaw the ramifications of a *Goodridge* -like ruling in 1997 when it passed the federal Defense of Marriage Act, which expressly authorizes states to refuse to recognize same-sex marriages even if they are valid in the state where they were performed. And, even if the Defense of Marriage Act were at some point overturned, for over a century states have been permitted to refuse to recognize certain marriages—those between first cousins, say—that are valid in the state of the ceremony but inconsistent with their own public policy.

The *Goodridge* ruling makes sense in large part because it stems directly from Massachusetts law. But it also makes sense because of the moral issue it addresses: the right of gays and lesbians to participate in one of society's most important and cherished institutions. Civil marriage is the principal means by which people publicly affirm their commitment to one another, but its legal and social effects are much broader than that. Let there be no confusion on this point: Marriage is an institution created by governments, not by nature. (Some opponents of gay marriage emphasize that marriage is created and sanctified by God; but we are speaking here of civil marriages, not religious ones.) Its benefits are intensely material as well as symbolic, including rights to insurance benefits, health coverage in the event of death of a spouse, generally lower tax rates, hospital visitation in the event of serious illness, and many more.

Celebrate Federalism

The Massachusetts court was correct to say that the "marriage ban works a deep and scarring hardship on a very real segment of the community." In an important and even daily sense, the prohibition on same-sex marriage turns gays and

113

lesbians into second-class citizens. There is thus a moral as well as a legal foundation for the *Goodridge* decision. Under the Massachusetts constitution, as under the U.S. Constitution, the core goal of the equality principle is to prevent the government from creating a caste system. As Justice John Harlan wrote in his lonely dissent to *Plessy v. Ferguson*, which found that providing separate facilities to segregate blacks was constitutional, "there is no caste" in America. The ban on same-sex marriage seems to violate that principle. Massachusetts Justice John M. Greaney, concurring separately in *Goodridge*, made this point explicitly, complaining of the "continued maintenance of this caste-like system."

Plausible as I find these arguments, however, they of course command nothing like universal agreement. But therein lies the beauty of *Goodridge:* To approve of it, it isn't necessary to be convinced that same-sex unions are legitimate and should be legalized across the country. It is necessary only to acknowledge that ours is a federal system and that reasonable people have made reasonable claims on behalf of those unions. In the 2000 campaign, Dick Cheney wisely emphasized that "different states are likely to come to different conclusions, and that's appropriate. I don't think there should necessarily be a federal policy in this area." Other states need not follow the route of *Goodridge*, but, regardless of how they resolve the issue, their choices will now be more informed, having had the opportunity to observe how well same-sex unions work in Massachusetts. Many Americans are seeing the *Goodridge* decision as a stirring tribute to individual rights. But, equally important, it is a remarkable tribute to U.S. federalism. We should celebrate it as such.

Federal Drug Laws Trump State Statutes

Jan Crawford Greenburg

The tug-of-war between state and federal power that was a subject of debate during the Constitutional Convention remains a point of contention in the twenty-first century. When state and federal laws are in conflict with one another, debate about state sovereignty and federal authority is often reopened. The following newspaper article by Jan Crawford Greenburg highlights a recent Supreme Court case in which state and federal laws clashed. In Raich v. Ashcroft, *California laws allowing the medical use of marijuana came in conflict with the Controlled Substances Act, a federal antidrug law.*

The Supreme Court ruled 6-3 that the federal government had the authority to enforce the Controlled Substances Act against people using marijuana for medical purposes despite the fact that state law permitted such drug use. Like previous Supreme Court cases involving states' rights, Raich v. Ashcroft *was based on the Court's interpretation of the commerce clause of the Constitution. The Court ruled that even though marijuana was not being transported from state to state, the federal government was authorized to regulate its production and use because it affected interstate commerce.*

Jan Crawford Greenburg of the Chicago Tribune *is a law journalist who reports about Supreme Court cases and national legal affairs. She is also a Supreme Court case analyst for* NewsHour with Jim Lehrer.

Terminally ill patients who smoke marijuana to alleviate pain can be prosecuted for violating federal drug laws, even if their own state laws allow them to use marijuana for medical purposes, the Supreme Court ruled Monday [June 6, 2005].

Federal Drug Laws Come First

In a 6-3 decision, the court ruled that federal drug laws, which say marijuana has no medical value, trump statutes in 11 states that allowed terminally ill patients to use the drug or limit penalties for doing so. Although the ruling does not overturn the state laws, it means patients who use marijuana for medical reasons could be arrested and prosecuted under the federal Controlled Substances Act.

Angel Raich, the 39-year-old California woman at the center of the case who uses marijuana to alleviate chronic pain, said Monday she would continue to use the drug and that she expected others in her situation to do so. She and other advocates said they would intensify efforts to lobby Congress to change federal drug laws, although Congress has shown no such inclination.

"If I stop using cannabis, unfortunately, I would die," said Raich, who suffers from wasting disease and joint pain.

The decision, written by Justice John Paul Stevens, acknowledged the "troubling facts" of the case and Raich's "strong arguments" that she will suffer irreparable harm without the benefits of marijuana.

But the issue before the court was whether Congress had power to regulate medical marijuana, not "whether it is wise to enforce the statute in these circumstances," Stevens wrote.

The Reach of Federal Power

In ruling against the terminally ill patients, the court strongly reaffirmed a broad scope of congressional power to regulate interstate commerce—even of products that are grown and consumed in the same state. Moreover, the court said that if it had ruled that Congress could not outlaw medical marijuana,

Kay Mitchell, 82, is a medical marijuana patient. She is protesting against the Justice Department's recent raids of medical marijuana dispensaries.© Kim Kulish/CORBIS

such a decision would surely have extended to homegrown marijuana used for recreational purposes as well.

The case was one of the most closely watched of the term, not only because of the practical implications in states with medical marijuana laws, but also because it involved deciding the extent of congressional power.

The decision produced an unusual line-up of liberal and conservative justices and makes clear the court sees real limits to a series of rulings in the last decade that have sharply curtailed Congress' power as it relates to the states.

"This is a case simply about the reach of federal power," said Randy Barnett, a law professor at Boston University School of Law who argued the case for Raich and another terminally ill California woman, Diane Monson.

Robert Raich, a lawyer and the husband of Angel Raich, said he did not expect the court's decision to have a broad practical impact, because the vast majority of marijuana prosecutions are at the state and local level. He said advocates would urge Congress to change the law to reflect marijuana's medicinal value.

In seeking to head off a federal prosecution, Raich and Monson had argued that Congress had no authority to ban their use of medical marijuana because the drug was grown solely for their own use and didn't leave the state of California. As such, it didn't concern interstate commerce and was not within Congress' power to regulate, they argued.

But the Justice Department contended that even marijuana grown solely for personal medical use could affect commerce and that Congress therefore had power to regulate it, under the Constitution's commerce clause.

Balance of Power a Key Issue

The balance of power between Congress and the states is an issue that has captivated this court in recent years and sharply divided the justices. In a series of opinions dating back more than a decade, the justices have generally divided 5-4, with the five conservatives in the majority, to put limits on Congress' power to pass laws governing many areas of American life.

But in Monday's case, two of those five, Justices Anthony Kennedy and Antonin Scalia, sided with their more liberal colleagues to uphold Congress' power to regulate medical marijuana use. Scalia wrote a separate opinion, in which he concurred with the outcome and said he saw the case as a straightforward one.

In his opinion for the majority, Stevens strongly reaffirmed a 1942 case on the scope of congressional power under the commerce clause. That case, which said Congress could regulate a farmer's wheat production that was grown solely for his family's use, was considered by critics as the most extreme validation of congressional power under the commerce clause.

"The hopes of those who wanted a fundamental rethinking of congressional power under the commerce clause are dashed—more even than they might have feared," said University of Chicago Law School professor Cass Sunstein.

Role of Commerce Power

The court said that the similarities between the wheat case and the medical marijuana issue were "striking." While neither product was produced for sale, the court said, Congress still could regulate them because of its interest in protecting or policing interstate markets in the products.

"In both cases, the regulation is squarely within Congress' commerce power because production of the commodity meant for home consumption, be it wheat or marijuana, has a substantial effect on supply and demand in the national market for the commodity," Stevens wrote for the court.

Justice Sandra Day O'Connor wrote a sharp dissent, joined by Chief Justice William Rehnquist and Clarence Thomas, in which she accused the majority of trivializing past decisions that have curbed the scope of federal power. O'Connor said the decision "stifles an express choice by some states, concerned for the lives and liberties of their people, to regulate medical marijuana differently."

The 11 states that allow medical marijuana usage or limit the penalty for such use are California, Maryland, Alaska, Colorado, Hawaii, Maine, Montana, Nevada, Oregon, Vermont and Washington.

The marijuana case came about after federal agents seized six marijuana plants from the backyard of Monson, who is 47 and suffering from spine disease. She, Raich and two of Raich's caregivers sued to block the federal government from enforcing the federal drug laws against them.

The U.S. Court of Appeals from the 9th Circuit agreed that Congress lacked the authority to subject them to federal drug laws because their activity did not involve interstate commerce.

Education Reform Sparks Debate over the Federal Government's Role

Alexandra Marks

The state-federal relationship encounters modern-day challenges not only in politics and commerce but also the social realm. Recently, the issue of education reform has illustrated a division in the way the federal government and some state governments believe such reform should be handled. More specifically, the No Child Left Behind Act (NCLB), signed by President George W. Bush in 2002, has sparked public debate on this subject. NCLB establishes federal standards and regulations for education; states are compelled to enact the reforms—which affect both teachers and students—necessary to achieve the NCLB goals. The federal government and the states in agreement with the NCLB mandate consider the reforms useful, effective, and within the jurisdiction of federal power. States in disagreement with NCLB dislike the idea of funding a federal mandate and the lack of local flexibility allowed by the law; they also resent federal involvement in what has traditionally been a state matter.

The following article by Alexandra Marks highlights the areas of discontent between the federal government and the states in rebellion against NCLB. Almost half of the fifty states are thinking of passing legislation that circumscribes or trumps the federal education law. Marks presents the opinions of federal and state government officials, school administrators, and education experts, all of whom weigh in on whether NCLB is a success or a failure in improving the education system. She reports that frus-

tration with the law is on the rise and that the states may push for adjustments to NCLB.

Alexandra Marks is a staff writer for the Christian Science Monitor.

Frustration with the federal No Child Left Behind education law is hitting new heights at the grass-roots level from Maine to California.

States in Rebellion

Three states are already in open rebellion: Connecticut, Utah, and Colorado, which have either planned lawsuits or passed laws that trump the federal mandates. At least five other states—Maine, Minnesota, Nevada, New Jersey, and Virginia—are deemed "hot spots" that could join the revolt.... And a total of 21 states are now considering some kind of legislation critical of No Child Left Behind (NCLB), according to a study ... by the Civil Society Institute, a nonpartisan advocacy group in Massachusetts.

It rounded up a report of this dissatisfaction to call attention to what it says is a disconnect between the federal government and the educators, students, parents, and local lawmakers that live with NCLB every day.

The law's supporters counter that it is working, with test scores going up. They acknowledge there's frustration, but they contend it has more to do with the level of federal intervention in what used to be a primarily state and local issue. They also praise the federal Department of Education (DOE) for being flexible in dealing with state concerns.

But several independent education experts, as well as state legislators from both the Republican and Democratic sides of the aisle, say that even with this flexibility, frustration is on the rise.

"There is a palpable increase in the level of dissatisfaction that I see, but it's not being translated into legislation in Congress," says Jack Jennings, president and CEO of the nonpartisan Center on Education Policy in Washington. "There's really a disjuncture here between a growing dissatisfaction and the lack of a political response."

Funding Federal Mandates

The frustration on the local level has to do with what educators call the rigidity of the law, which requires high-stakes, standardized testing and penalizes schools deemed as failing to make "adequate yearly progress." They're also concerned about a lack of funding to pay for the testing and the remedial services needed to ensure students make the grade.

For instance, Connecticut estimates it will cost the state $41.6 million more to implement NCLB than the federal government is providing. Local communities will bear additional costs, too.

The White House and the DOE dispute that. They point to two studies done by the Government Accountability Office in New Jersey and Massachusetts that found those states had enough federal resources to implement the law. They also note that since NCLB was passed, federal education spending has increased more than 30 percent.

"It is unfortunate that some appear to think that reform is more trouble than it's worth," says DOE spokeswoman Samara Yudof. "No Child Left Behind is working: Evidence from both the Nation's Report Card and the states' own data prove it."

Critism of NCLB

Although test scores are going up, they were before NCLB was passed, as well. That's because of state education reforms and testing protocols put into place over the past 25 years. Indeed, there's been no research to determine which reforms get credit for the increasing scores. But many teachers and local legislators credit the earlier state improvements, and they're concerned that NCLB mandates are actually undermining their students' long-term success.

They argue that the high-stakes nature of NCLB's test encourages "teaching to the test" and actually undermines learning and critical-thinking skills. At the same time, they contend, NCLB mandates drain resources from key enrichment programs.

"The consequences especially for minority students are more and more tragic, and you see it in the data," says Sylvia Bruni, assistant superintendent of the Laredo, Texas, Independent School District. "We have enormous dropout rates, in my community as many 30 percent of all students. . . . Statewide there's a marked decline in the number of students who are prepared for higher education."

Ms. Bruni says that one of the biggest indications of NCLB's failure comes from the business community, which has found that students are "graduating as poor communicators, really weak critical thinkers, weak problem solvers."

Proponents of NCLB

But other states and school districts maintain that the law is having its intended effect of raising not only test scores, but also students' overall preparedness for the global economy.

For example, every single jurisdiction in the state of Maryland improved in performance in the past year [2003–2004], according to State Superintendent of Schools Nancy Grasmick. She credits NCLB, which she says forces schools to be in a "mode of continual improvement, raising the bar."

"In the past, even in some of our best schools, we've hidden behind the averages, and there were children who were not making substantial progress," she says. "The law . . . now requires us to look at every subgroup. I actually think that's an extremely positive thing. We're never going to overcome an achievement gap . . . until we do this."

NCLB's advocates also note the DOE has reached out to states to understand their concerns. Of the 40 states that have asked for waivers recently, more than 35 have been granted, according to the DOE.

Adjusting the Law

But even strong supporters of the law say that some of the regulations "need adjustment" and more funding would be helpful. Superintendent Grasmick notes that part of Maryland's success was a result of the state legislature approving an additional $1.3 billion in funds to help implement the program over five years.

"I know that's not true in a lot of states," she says. "They've actually experienced cuts in funding."

Several US representatives and senators are reportedly working on bills to amend NCLB . . . , but few education experts believe it will happen before 2007, when the law comes up for reauthorization. But as the calls for change increase on the local level, that may change.

"I think the dissatisfaction will continue to grow," says Reggie Felton, director of federal relations with the National School Boards Association in Alexandria, Va. "That will result in a stronger sense of urgency in congressional districts, which will then result in members of Congress saying, 'We can't wait. We must act now because I'm up for reelection.'"

Appendix A

The Origins of the American Bill of Rights

The U.S. Constitution as it was originally created and submitted to the colonies for ratification in 1787 did not include what we now call the Bill of Rights. This omission was the cause of much controversy as Americans debated whether to accept the new Constitution and the new federal government it created. One of the main concerns voiced by opponents of the document was that it lacked a detailed listing of guarantees of certain fundamental individual rights. These critics did not succeed in preventing the Constitution's ratification, but were in large part responsible for the existence of the Bill of Rights.

In 1787 the United States consisted of thirteen former British colonies that had been loosely bound since 1781 by the Articles of Confederation. Since declaring their independence from Great Britain in 1776, the former colonies had established their own colonial governments and constitutions, eight of which had bills of rights written into them. One of the most influential was Virginia's Declaration of Rights. Drafted largely by planter and legislator George Mason in 1776, the seventeen-point document combined philosophical declarations of natural rights with specific limitations on the powers of government. It served as a model for other state constitutions.

The sources for these declarations of rights included English law traditions dating back to the 1215 Magna Carta and the 1689 English Bill of Rights—two historic documents that provided specific legal guarantees of the "true, ancient, and indubitable rights and liberties of the people" of England. Other legal sources included the colonies' original charters, which declared that colonists should have the same "privileges, franchises, and immunities" that they would if they lived in England. The ideas concerning natural rights developed by John Locke and other English philosophers were also influential. Some of these concepts of rights had been cited in the Declaration of Independence to justify the American Revolution.

Unlike the state constitutions, the Articles of Confederation, which served as the national constitution from 1781 to 1788, lacked a bill of rights. Because the national government under the Articles of Confederation had little authority by design, most people believed it posed little threat to civil liberties, rendering a bill of rights unnecessary. However, many influential leaders criticized the very weakness of the national government for creating its own problems; it did not create an effective system for conducting a coherent foreign policy, settling disputes between states, printing money, and coping with internal unrest.

It was against this backdrop that American political leaders convened in Philadelphia in May 1787 with the stated intent to amend the Articles of Confederation. Four months later the Philadelphia Convention, going beyond its original mandate, created a whole new Constitution with a stronger national government. But while the new Constitution included a few provisions protecting certain civil liberties, it did not include any language similar to Virginia's Declaration of Rights. Mason, one of the delegates in Philadelphia, refused to sign the document. He listed his objections in an essay that began:

> There is no Declaration of Rights, and the Laws of the general government being paramount to the laws and constitution of the several States, the Declaration of Rights in the separate States are no security.

Mason's essay was one of hundreds of pamphlets and other writings produced as the colonists debated whether to ratify the new Constitution (nine of the thirteen colonies had to officially ratify the Constitution for it to go into effect). The supporters of the newly drafted Constitution became known as Federalists, while the loosely organized group of opponents were called Antifederalists. Antifederalists opposed the new Constitution for several reasons. They believed the presidency would create a monar-

chy, Congress would not be truly representative of the people, and state governments would be endangered. However, the argument that proved most effective was that the new document lacked a bill of rights and thereby threatened Americans with the loss of cherished individual liberties. Federalists realized that to gain the support of key states such as New York and Virginia, they needed to pledge to offer amendments to the Constitution that would be added immediately after its ratification. Indeed, it was not until this promise was made that the requisite number of colonies ratified the document. Massachusetts, Virginia, South Carolina, New Hampshire, and New York all included amendment recommendations as part of their decisions to ratify.

One of the leading Federalists, James Madison of Virginia, who was elected to the first Congress to convene under the new Constitution, took the lead in drafting the promised amendments. Under the process provided for in the Constitution, amendments needed to be passed by both the Senate and House of Representatives and then ratified by three-fourths of the states. Madison sifted through the suggestions provided by the states and drew upon the Virginia Declaration of Rights and other state documents in composing twelve amendments, which he introduced to Congress in September 1789. "If they are incorporated into the constitution," he argued in a speech introducing his proposed amendments,

> Independent tribunals of justice will consider themselves in a peculiar manner the guardians of those rights; they will be an impenetrable bulwark against every assumption of power in the legislative or executive; they will be naturally led to resist every encroachment upon rights expressly stipulated for in the constitution by the declaration of rights.

After debate and some changes to Madison's original proposals, Congress approved the twelve amendments and sent them to the states for ratification. Two amendments were not ratified; the remaining ten became known as the Bill of Rights. Their ratification by the states was completed on December 15, 1791.

Appendix B

Supreme Court Cases Involving States' Rights

1819
McCulloch v. Maryland

The Court declared the constitutionality of a national bank under the "elastic clause" of the Constitution, which gives Congress the authority to make laws necessary to carry out the work of the federal government. It also found that states do not have the right to tax the federal government.

1824
Gibbons v. Ogden

The Court ruled that it is not unconstitutional for Congress to regulate activities affecting interstate commerce and that federal law takes precedence over state law.

1861
Kentucky v. Dennison

The Court held that a state governor cannot be coerced by federal power into returning a fugitive from justice to another state.

1870
Collector v. Day

The Court deemed it unconstitutional to levy a national income tax on the salaries of state officials.

1890
Hans v. Louisiana

The Court ruled that states cannot be sued by their own citizens in federal court.

1896

Plessy v. Ferguson

The Court declared that states have the right to pass laws that require segregation of the races in separate railroad cars despite the Fourteenth Amendment's guarantee of equal rights for all citizens.

1903

Champion v. Ames

The Court found that due to its interstate commerce authority, Congress may prohibit the carrying or trafficking of lottery tickets from one state to another.

1911

Hipolite Egg Co. v. United States

Citing congressional authority to regulate interstate commerce, the Court upheld the federal government's power to confiscate contaminated food after it has been shipped between states.

1918

Hammer v. Dagenhart

The Court struck down the Keating-Owen Child Labor Act of 1916, stating that it violated states' rights as defined by the Tenth Amendment.

1931

United States v. Sprague

The Court denied the appeal of a defendant indicted under the Eighteenth Amendment, which prohibited alcohol sale and distribution between 1919 and 1933. The defendant claimed that the Eighteenth Amendment's ratification by state legislatures rather than constitutional convention was invalid.

1939

Graves v. O'Keefe

The Court overturned the *Collector v. Day* (1870) decision and ruled that a state can levy a nondiscriminatory income tax on the salary of a state government employee.

1941
United States v. Darby

The Court unanimously upheld the Fair Labor Standards Act of 1938, which regulated wages and hours, as a means of congressional authority to regulate interstate commerce. The ruling also overturned the *Hammer v. Dagenhart* (1918) decision.

1942
Wickard v. Filburn

In a case that marks the greatest expansion of federal authority under the commerce clause of the Constitution, the Court found that interstate commerce regulation may be extended to include the production of goods as well as their transport and sale.

1946
Testa v. Katt

The Court ruled that Congress can require state courts to consider legal action relevant to federal law.

1968
Maryland v. Wirtz

The Court declared that the Fair Labor Standards Act of 1938 applied not only to federal employees but also to state employees.

1970
Oregon v. Mitchell

The Court placed limits on congressional authority by ruling that the minimum voting age could be lowered to eighteen for national elections but that states can determine the voting age for state elections.

1975

Fry v. United States

The Court upheld regulation allowing Congress to freeze the wages of state employees as an emergency measure to counter severe inflation in the national economy.

1976

National League of Cities v. Usery

Overturning *Maryland v. Wirtz* (1968) and reviving *Hammer v. Dagenhart* (1918), the Court ruled that the Fair Labor Standards Act of 1938 does not cover state and municipal employees. Congress cannot legislate on minimum wage for employees in these categories.

1982

FERC v. Mississippi

The Court declared that Congress can require state public utility commissions to consider claims based on certain federal regulations.

1985

Garcia v. San Antonio Metropolitan Transit Authority

The Court overruled *National League of Cities v. Usery* (1976). The ruling signified that states (and state employees) must comply with federal laws.

1987

Puerto Rico v. Branstad

The Court overturned the decision reached in *Kentucky v. Dennison* (1918) and permitted governors to enforce the return of a fugitive from justice who has escaped to another state.

1992

New York v. United States

The Court found that the federal government cannot directly compel a state to enforce or enact a federal regulatory program.

1995
United States v. Lopez

The Court struck down the Gun-Free School Zones Act of 1990, which prohibited firearm possession in a school zone, because it violated states' rights and could not be considered a form of interstate commerce regulation allowed by the Constitution's commerce clause.

1997
Printz v. United States

The Court ruled that Congress lacks the authority to override state legislatures by requiring local background checks for handgun ownership, which was a provision of the Brady Handgun Violence Prevention Act.

2005
Raich v. Ashcroft

The Court declared that federal antidrug laws trump state laws legalizing the medicinal use of marijuana.

For Further Research

Books

Patrick T. Conley and John P. Kaminski, eds., *The Bill of Rights and the States*. Madison, WI: Madison House, 1992.

David P. Currie, *The Constitution in the Supreme Court*. Chicago: University of Chicago Press, 1990.

John D. Donahue, *Disunited States*. New York: BasicBooks, 1997.

Frederick D. Drake and Lynn R. Nelson, eds., *States' Rights and American Federalism: A Documentary History*. Westport, CT: Greenwood, 1999.

Richard E. Ellis, *The Union at Risk*. New York: Oxford University Press, 1987.

Daniel Farber, *Lincoln's Constitution*. Chicago: University of Chicago Press, 2003.

Robert A. Goldwin, *A Nation of States: Essays on the American Federal System*. Chicago: Rand McNally, 1963.

Frank Goodman, *The Annals of the American Academy of Political and Social Science: The Supreme Court's Federalism: Real or Imagined?* Philadelphia: Sage, 2001.

Ronald Hoffman and Peter J. Albert, eds., *The Bill of Rights: Government Proscribed*. Charlottesville: University Press of Virginia, 1997.

Mark R. Killenbeck, ed., *The Tenth Amendment and State Sovereignty: Constitutional History and Contemporary Issues*. Lanham, MD: Rowman and Littlefield, 2002.

James J. Kilpatrick, *The Sovereign States: Notes of a Citizen of Virginia*. Chicago: Henry Regnery, 1957.

Jon Kukla, ed., *The Bill of Rights: A Lively Heritage*. Richmond: Virginia State Library and Archives, 1987.

Forrest McDonald, *States' Rights and the Union: Imperium in Imperio, 1776–1876*. Lawrence: University Press of Kansas, 2000.

Kevin T. McGuire, *Understanding the U.S. Supreme Court: Cases and Controversies*. Boston: McGraw-Hill, 2001.

Louis H. Pollak, ed., *The Constitution and the Supreme Court*. Vols. 1, 2. Cleveland, OH: World, 1966.

M.N.S. Sellers, *American Republicanism: Roman Ideology in the United States Constitution*. New York: New York University Press, 1994.

Clyde N. Wilson and W. Edwin Hemphill, eds., *The Papers of John C. Calhoun*. Vol. 10. Columbia: University of South Carolina Press, 1977.

Periodicals

Ann Althouse, "Vanguard States, Laggard States: Federalism and Constitutional Rights," *University of Pennsylvania Law Review*, June 2004.

Brannon P. Denning and Jack H. McCall, "States' Rights and Foreign Policy: Some Things Should Be Left to Washington," *Foreign Affairs*, January/February 2000.

John D. Donahue, "The Disunited States: 'Devolution'— Shifting Power from Washington to the Fifty States—Is No Cure for What Ails American Government," *Atlantic Monthly*, May 1997.

Laura S. Jensen, "Federal Authority vs. State Autonomy: The Supreme Court's Role Revisited," *Public Administration Review*, March 1999.

Alex Kreit, "The Future of Medical Marijuana: Should the States Grow Their Own?" *University of Pennsylvania Law Review*, May 2003.

Paul Magnusson, "States Rights vs. Free Trade: As Trade Pacts Proliferate, States Start to Howl About Lost Sovereignty," *Business Week*, March 2005.

Ann McColl, "Tough Call—Is No Child Left Behind Constitutional?" *Phi Delta Kappan*, April 2005.

Patricia T. Northrop, "The Constitutional Insignificance of Funding for Federal Mandates," *Duke Law Journal*, February 1997.

Edward L. Rubin, "If the States Had Been Sovereign," *Constitutional Commentary*, Winter 1999.

David G. Savage, "Federalism and the Supreme Court," *State Legislatures*, October/November 2001.

———, "High Court Decisions Mixed for States," *State Legislatures*, September 2000.

Denise Scheberle, "Partners in Policymaking: Forging Effective Federal-State Relations," *Environment*, December 1998.

Mary M. Timney, "Short Circuit: Federal-State Relations in the California Energy Crisis," *Publius*, Fall 2002.

Dane Waters, "States' Rights and the Initiative Process," *Campaigns and Elections*, April 2002.

Regina Werum, "Sectionalism and Racial Politics: Federal Vocational Policies and Programs in the Predesegregation South," *Social Science History*, Autumn 1997.

Charles Wise, "Judicial Federalism: The Resurgence of the Supreme Court's Role in the Protection of State Sovereignty," *Public Administration Review*, March/April 1998.

Timothy Zick, "Statehood as the New Personhood: The Discovery of Fundamental States' Rights," *William and Mary Law Review*, October 2004.

Web Sites

Exploring Constitutional Law (www.law.umkc.edu/faculty/
projects/ftrials/conlaw/home.html). This site by Doug
Linder explores legal controversies and issues surrounding
the U.S. Constitution. It includes discussion of the commerce clause and the Tenth Amendment and how they
relate to states' rights.

FindLaw (www.findlaw.com). This site offers the complete
text of Supreme Court rulings as well as legal news and
commentary.

Landmark Supreme Court Cases (www.landmarkcases.org).
This site, sponsored by Street Law and the Supreme
Court Historical Society, highlights landmark Supreme
Court cases via background summaries and majority and
minority opinion excerpts. The site is geared toward the
teaching of these cases and contains supplementary activities as well.

Index